Posh

Laura Wade is an Olivier-award winning playwright and screenwriter. Her play *Home, I'm Darling* premiered at Theatr Clwyd in 2018 before playing at the National Theatre and won the award for Best New Comedy at the 2019 Oliviers. In 2018 she adapted Jane Austen's unfinished novel *The Watsons* for the stage for Chichester Festival Theatre. In 2015 she adapted Sarah Waters's *Tipping the Velvet* for the stage and it premiered at the Lyric Hammersmith before transferring to the Royal Lyceum in Edinburgh. Her screenplay *The Riot Club*, an adaptation of her 2010 stage play *Posh*, premiered at Toronto International Film Festival 2014 and opened in cinemas on September 2014. *Posh* opened in the West End at the Duke of York's Theatre in 2012 after its premiere at the Royal Court Theatre in April 2010.

Henry Bell is a Senior Lecturer in Performance at University of the West of Scotland, UK where he fulfils the role of Arts Lead in the Division of Arts and Media. Prior to entering full time in academia in 2016, he worked as a professional theatre director and applied theatre practitioner predominantly at the Orange Tree Theatre (Community, Education and Literary Director 2009–2013) and Stephen Joseph Theatre (Associate Director 2013–2016). His written research has been published in the *Journal for Research in Drama Education* (RiDE), *Theatre, Dance and Performance Training and Shakespeare Bulletin*. Practice-as-Research outputs have taken place at the Biennale di Venezia (2017), War Childhood Museum (Sarajevo) and he is co-founder of the Decentred Shakespeares Network researching and creating practice in Scotland, Ghana, Brazil, India and South Africa.

Posh

LAURA WADE

With commentary and notes by

HENRY BELL

Series Editors: Jenny Stevens, Matthew Nichols,
Sara Freeman and Chris Megson

methuen | drama

LONDON · NEW YORK · OXFORD · NEW DELHI · SYDNEY

METHUEN DRAMA
Bloomsbury Publishing Plc
50 Bedford Square, London, WC1B 3DP, UK
1385 Broadway, New York, NY 10018, USA
29 Earlsfort Terrace, Dublin 2, Ireland

BLOOMSBURY, METHUEN DRAMA and the Methuen Drama logo are
trademarks of Bloomsbury Publishing Plc

First published in Great Britain by Oberon Books 2010
Reprinted by Methuen Drama 2021 and 2022
This edition published by Methuen Drama 2024

Posh © 2010
Commentary and Notes © Henry Bell, 2024

The playtext in this edition includes changes to the text from the 2012 production
at the Duke of York's.

Cover design: Eleanor Rose
Cover image © Vince Cavataio/Getty Images

A catalogue record for this book is available from the British Library.

ISBN: PB: 978-1-3502-3576-2
       ePDF: 978-1-3502-3577-9
       eBook: 978-1-3502-3578-6

Series: Student Editions

Typeset by RefineCatch Limited, Bungay, Suffolk
Printed and bound in India

To find out more about our authors and books visit www.bloomsbury.com
and sign up for our newsletters.

Contents

Contents

Introduction

Chronology

Harvey, is professionally produced at Bristol Old Vic Basement (2000). Wade begins a three-year working relationship with Playbox Theatre. Writes unpublished plays, *The Wild Swans* (2000), *TwelveMachine* (2001) and *The Last Child* (2002) during this period.

2001   7 June – David Cameron and Boris Johnson both elected as Conservative MPs for the first time.

2003   Laura Wade joins the Royal Court Young Writers' Group. Begins writing *Colder Than Here*.

2 December – Wade's adaptation of W. H. Auden's *Young Emma*, directed by Tamara Harvey, opens at the Finborough Theatre, London.

2004   Wade becomes Writer-in-Residence at Finborough Theatre, London.

2005   3 February – *Colder Than Here,* directed by Abigail Morris, opens at Soho Theatre, London.

24 February – *Breathing Corpses*, directed by Anna Mackmin, opens at the Royal Court Jerwood Theatre Upstairs. The play later wins the Pearson Playwrights' Best Play Award and is the joint winner of the George Devine Award.

Wade wins Critics' Circle Theatre Award for Most Promising Playwright for both *Colder Than Here* and *Breathing Corpses*.

3 December – Four Bullingdon Club members arrested as 17 bottles of wine and 'every piece of crockery and a window' are smashed at the fifteenth-century pub, The White Hart, in Fyfield, Oxfordshire.

6 December – David Cameron becomes leader of the Conservative Party.

2006   15 February – *Other Hands* opens at Soho Theatre, London. Directed by Bijan Shebani, cast includes Katherine Parkinson.

Catch opens at the Royal Court Theatre, London. Co-authored by Wade and April de Angelis, Stella Feehily, Tanika Gupta, and Chloe Moss.

2010   9 April – *Posh* opens at Royal Court Theatre, London. Directed by Lyndsey Turner. Cast includes a young Kit Harington and James Norton. The play quickly sells out and is one of the most successful box office productions in the Royal Court's history.

6 May – Following a General Election, David Cameron becomes Prime Minister of the United Kingdom as a coalition government of the Conservative Party and Liberal Democrats ousts Gordon Brown's Labour Party.

17 June – *Alice*, Wade's adaptation of Lewis Carroll's *Alice in Wonderland*, opens at the Crucible, Sheffield. Directed by Lyndsey Turner.

2012   23 May – *Posh* opens at Duke of York's Theatre, London. Directed by Lyndsey Turner with an updated script.

2014   *The Riot Club*, a film adaptation of *Posh*, is released. Directed by Lone Scherfig, from a screenplay by Laura Wade.

2015   Boris Johnson elected as MP for Uxbridge and South Ruislip.

Regional premiere of *Posh*, co-produced by Nottingham Playhouse and Salisbury Playhouse, directed by Susannah Tresilian.

2017   All-female production of *Posh*, directed by Cressida Carré, opens at the Pleasance Theatre, London.

Historical, social and cultural contexts

The first preview of *Posh* took place on 9 April 2010 almost exactly thirteen years into the centre-left Labour Party's period of governance. Less than a month after the opening of the play, Labour lost the 2010 General Election and the new right-wing Conservative/ Liberal Democrat coalition government began:

> Then when the great New Labour shop in the sky goes up in flames 'cause it turns out there *isn't* an endless supply of toys and sweets [...] They vote *us* back in to sort it all out, make it all go away.
>
> Alistair (95–96)

It may come as a surprise to learn that *Posh* was written in 2010 while Britain was still governed by the Labour Party. This New Labour movement, conceived by Tony Blair and Gordon Brown, won a historic General Election in 1997 ending 18 years of Conservative Government. Blair's manifesto made several pledges in relation to addressing social inequality.

> I want a Britain that is one nation, with shared values and purpose, where merit comes before privilege, run for the many not the few, strong and sure of itself at home and abroad.[1]

The political landscape from 1997 to 2010 saw many 'centre-left', 'socialist soft' policies directed at alleviating the UK's unequal society. Initiatives such as the New Deal, Welfare to Work, and the introduction of the minimum wage focused on creating a social landscape in which there was a 'safety net' to support people but also offer tangible routes to get people into work and respond to the rapid change from an industrial to post-industrial society. When Alistair's monologue at the end of Act 1 ends 'I'm sick to fucking death of poor people', (90) we start to understand the Riot Club's opposition to this political movement which, to them, unfairly favoured people they considered to be underprivileged. As Wade stated in a *Guardian* interview in 2014, 'The 2010 production had the boys living under a Labour government and feeling like their backs were up against the wall because of that'.[2] Alistair's

---

[1]   Tony Blair. *New Labour, Because Britain Deserves Better.* Labour Party, 1997.
[2]   Emine Saner. 'The Posh Club'. *The Guardian.* 21 September 2014.

perspective on these policies is made explicitly clear at the beginning of Act 2, 'Blair's lot, giving the kids too much pocket money' (93).

Behind the scenes[3]

Laura Wade: Some early scenes that I wrote while developing the form of the play were inspired by the idea of a posh boy who had lived his whole life in a country house with portraits of his ancestors on the walls, looking down at him in disappointment. In a very early version we had a Lord Riot type character in the same scenario as the gentlemen's club at the beginning of the play. The ancestor was sitting in an armchair across from the young guy telling him something like 'your generation are disappointing to me. You've thrown it all away. Look at all the power we had and now you've spaffed it up the wall'.

The broader political context, involving the shift to the right in UK politics, is at the heart of *Posh* but Wade also responds to the changing demographics of politicians in the United Kingdom during the 2000s. Three years before the first performance of *Posh*, on 13 February 2007, the *Mail on Sunday* published the annual photo of the 1987 Bullingdon Club which hitherto had not been available to the public.[4] This depicted ten young men in formal tailcoats posing in front of Christchurch, Oxford and included both David Cameron and Boris Johnson, future prime ministers of the UK. The publication was highly embarrassing for Cameron who had just become leader of the Conservative Party and was looking to challenge the ruling Labour Party at the next general election.

Looking back at the photograph in 2019, Cameron remarked,

When I look now at the much-reproduced photograph taken of our group of appallingly over-self-confident 'sons of

---

[3]   The *Behind the scenes* text boxes contain material from a new interview with Laura Wade, conducted by Henry Bell in July 2022.

[4]   'Cameron's Cronies in the Bullingdon Class of '87'. *Daily Mail*. 13 February 2007.

privilege', I cringe. If I had known at the time the grief I would get for that picture, of course I would never have joined. But life isn't like that.[5]

In 2007, Cameron was attempting to move the public conception of the Conservative Party away from its previous reputation as being the 'Nasty Party' with roots in the more privileged demographics of the UK. Beyond the 1987 photograph, stories also began to emerge about the behaviour of that generation of 'Bullers'. Many of these stories are collected in Simon Kuper's 2022 book on the influence of Oxford University on twenty-first-century UK politics, *Chums*. Kuper discusses a 1987 incident involving David Cameron and Boris Johnson when several Bullingdon members were arrested after somebody threw a plant pot through a restaurant window. Johnson later claimed,

> The party ended up with a number of us crawling on all fours through the hedges of the Botanical Gardens, and trying to escape police dogs. And once we were in the cells, we became pathetic namby-pambies.[6]

One club member who was arrested said later that Johnson's claims to have been held overnight at Cowley police station were untruthful boasts. The same man identifies the only three members who escaped arrest that night: Johnson, Cameron (who had run off down a side street), and their fellow Old Etonian Sebastian Grigg, now Fourth Baron Altrincham.

Behind the scenes

Henry Bell: Why did you make it The Riot Club rather than The Bullingdon Club?

[5]   David Cameron. 'David Cameron Book: the truth about me, cannabis and Eton'. *Times*. 14 September 2019.

[6]   Simon Kuper. *Chums. How a Tiny Caste of Oxford Tories Took Over the UK*. London: Profile Books, 2022. pp. 52–3.

> Laura Wade: Partly because I didn't want it to be about skewering specific people because that would limit it. It was more about an attitude. And an attitude in a metaphorical sense in that it was about an entire class of people and their behaviour towards the rest of the country. Not just the boys in the club.
>
> As a writer, I enjoy creating a world. I enjoy inventing rules and a language. Creating the club was really fun. We did some initial workshops with actors where we asked, 'what would this club do? What would the rules be? What would the attitudes be? What are the rituals that they perform at these dinners?' It was just much more fun to devise our own than try to find out what the actual boys actually did.

This sort of behaviour and the 1987 photograph served as a reminder of the discrepancy between David Cameron's attempt to clean up the Conservative Party's image, and the truth of their privileged backgrounds. Wade's play puts the audience in a private space where the prejudices, codes and behaviours of this social group are laid bare.

Though Oxford is full of students that do not share the background or the opinions of Wade's fictional dining society, those invited to join the Bullingdon invariably come from the UK's major public schools. The Riot Club mirrors the educational and political trajectory of Conservative figures of the 2010s like Cameron, Johnson and Jacob Rees-Mogg: Eton – Oxford – Oxford Union – Conservative Party – (and in two cases) Prime Minister.

It is important to draw attention to the continued behaviour of the Bullingdon Club in the build up to the creation of *Posh*. The club attracted notoriety in 2005, when a fifteenth-century pub in Oxfordshire was vandalized and Bullingdon members attempted to bribe staff. Four members were arrested and an Oxford University student paper printed an interview with an anonymous member of the club who gave details about the £10,000 joining fee and the club motto, 'I like the sound of breaking glass'.[7]

---

[7] Sophie McBain. 'Smashing Job Chaps: An Inside Look at The Bullingdon Club'. *Oxford Student*. 12 January 2005.

Behind the scenes

Laura Wade: The 2005 incident was my lightbulb moment because that felt like such a perfect metaphor for the behaviour of a certain class of people. That it's OK to smash things up and behave as badly as you want as long as you can afford to pay for it afterwards. That felt like a very dramatic and quite dangerous idea that was worth poking at.

According to some commentators, *Posh* had an impact on Bullingdon Club membership and activities. In 2017, youth media site The Tab published a video showing the club's annual photograph at Christchurch being cancelled by a university Porter.[8] In a further blow, the Oxford University Conservative Association (OUCA, mentioned in *Posh*), banned its members from joining the club in 2018.

Genre and themes

Is *Posh* an example of realism? Is it a satire? Is it a State of the Nation play? Is it all three? Laura Wade's writing is difficult to define in terms of genre, but many of the most exciting plays have that in common.

Is Posh an example of realism?

Realism tends to manifest in three ways. First, there is the commitment to representing everyday life on stage in how people speak and move. Second, a realistic play is one in which people's actions are a product of their environment and upbringing. Third, realism presents a stage picture which is a recognizable depiction of

---

[8] Lucy Habron. 'The Bullingdon Club Got Kicked Out Of Christ Church Trying To Take Their Annual Photo'. *The Oxford Tab*. 29 June 2017.

the material world. These three characteristics do not exist independently, they influence each other.

Posh is written almost entirely in a realistic style. The dialogue is sharp and well observed with specific slang and references to the demographic of the people depicted. An example of this occurs early on, when Jeremy asks Guy if he is 'Playing any rugger?' (6). Wade deliberately uses as realistic a term as possible, which might not be understandable to some people reading or watching the play. The word 'rugger' identifies Jeremy and Guy as being from a specific background as does their environment and physical attitude to it, described by Wade as 'A Gentlemen's Club in London. A wood-panelled room with two big leather armchairs and a small table between them' (5). This is a familiar setting for men educated at exclusive and expensive schools: it is a comfortable environment and the conversation that ensues is honest – Jeremy is happy to discuss confidential matters whilst 'sipping from a glass of whisky' (5).

As the action of the play moves to the Bull's Head, the characters' attitude to space changes. At the climax of the play, the vandalism carried out in the pub's reception room can be seen as a product of the characters' upbringing and their attitude to their location. The play leads its audience to ask: what is this upbringing that has such a destructive effect on the physical environment in which the characters spend most of the play?

The English independent school system plays a key part in the backgrounds of most characters in *Posh*. Almost all the ten-strong Riot Club attended a private school, and while it is not made explicit through a close reading of the text it can be deduced that the majority attended one of the most exclusive private schools in the world, Eton College, and were educated as part of an all-male cohort.

The key theme of privilege is, in part, enabled by Wade's psychological exploration of the Riot Club's behaviour. For Wade, this approach is vital to the success of a production.

Behind the scenes

Laura Wade: The first thing I always say to any group I talk to who are approaching the play: don't send them up. You don't need to add things to make them funny, the script will be more funny if you embody them earnestly. You're not playing a caricature, you're playing a person. And you don't need to show your disapproval for the boys through your performance, either. The characters' actions will do that for you. So don't comment, imagine what it's like to be them, feeling entitled to do everything they do without shame or self-doubt.

A final example of *Posh*'s realist credentials can be found in the association between the prejudiced language and behaviour of the Riot Club and their schooling and background. The first time a woman is mentioned at the Riot Club's gathering is by Harry as he describes an encounter he has just had with an unnamed female attendee at a fencing match (19). His description uses sexualized language to dehumanize the woman involved: 'a blowjob's a blowjob' (19). Harry's sex act gives him a twisted sense of victory over the captain of the rival fencing club at Cambridge University. In a trend that will continue throughout the play, this behaviour is not challenged by Harry's contemporaries in the Riot Club – far from it, Harry is considered by his peers to be the member most suited to female interaction. This unchecked misogyny leads to an escalation of language and attitudes which results in the assault of Rachel towards the end of Act 2.

This assault is rooted in the conditions in which people from the socio-economic background of the Riot Club are educated. In February 2021, the Head Prefect at the private Cranbrook school, Asher Learmonth, wrote an open letter to his contemporaries at the school which connects directly to much of the behaviour of the Riot Club in *Posh*. He wrote that 'there have been times when I've heard about disgusting behaviour and not done anything about it, times when I've tolerated boys referring to women in derogatory ways . . .

times when I've stood by'.[9] Learmonth considers a single-sex education, such as that experienced by most of the Riot Club, as a key part in this:

> You wouldn't study with them [women] for example or play sport together, you wouldn't have dinners with their family when your parents are away. No. They're people you see once a week. From the hours of 7–11 on a Saturday night. In a completely artificial environment.[10]

In a UK context, the misogyny of boys at Eton College became a national news story in 2022 when girls from a non-fee paying state school attended a talk by right-wing politician, Nigel Farage. According to the BBC, girls were 'booed' and 'subjected to misogynistic language and racial slurs' from the male pupils of Eton.[11] This is another example of the isolated, boarding school experience, in a single sex education context, that leads to outward displays of prejudice. The objectification of women in the play is explained by the characters' lack of prolonged contact outside of limited social settings. Not all pupils of all-boys schools go on to hold the views and use the language that the Riot Club uses in relation to women but a consideration of their formative environments is essential to an understanding of the play.

Is Posh an example of satire?

In 2014, Wade explained that a key question behind the play was, 'What makes people behave like that?'[12] and satire often utilizes a different toolkit from realism to explore such questions on stage. As definitions of this term suggest, 'Satire uses various types of comic exaggeration to ridicule human institutions or behaviour, in the hope of their being changed or corrected'.[13] While it is important to

---

[9]   Asher Learmonth. 'Our boys' treatment of girls has been disgusting: Cranbrook prefect pleads for respect'. *Sydney Morning Herald*. 25 February 2021.

[10] Ibid.

[11] Robin Brant. 'Eton College boys 'booed' visiting state schoolgirls'. *BBC News*. 18 November 2022.

[12] Emine Saner. 'The Posh Club'. *The Guardian*. 21 September 2014.

[13] Colin Chambers, ed. *The Continuum Companion to Twentieth Century Theatre*. London: Continuum, 2002. p. 669.

understand that much of the behaviour depicted in *Posh* can be justified entirely from a psychological perspective and bears close resemblance to real life events which have taken place and continue to take place, it is also prudent to acknowledge the satirical contents of the play.

The key aspect of satire in *Posh* is Lord Riot's appearance in Act Two (102).

Behind the scenes

Laura Wade: I think that the energy of the evening has summoned the spirit of Lord Riot. You just have to accept that, just for five minutes, we live in a world where that's possible.

Lord Riot is described by Wade as 'an eighteenth century libertine' (102) and his language, costume and body language are based on these social codes. He is not of the material world of the twenty-first century in which the play is set. *Posh* becomes satire when the Riot Club accepts this schism in their reality and, moreover, when the ridiculous figure of Lord Riot is adopted as a champion and potential 'saviour' from the perceived ills of the world by the young men on stage.

Is Posh a State of the Nation Play?

Arriving at a definition of a State of the Nation Play has challenged critics and theatre writers in the early twenty-first century. Matt Trueman, writing less than a year after *Posh* was first performed, questioned its very existence[14] whereas Michael Billington's 2007 history of post-war British Theatre is titled *State of Nation*. For Billington, 'What theatre can do is shift attitudes, articulate

---

[14]   Matt Trueman. 'There's no such thing as a state of the nation play'. *The Guardian*. 22 March, 2011.

discontent, and reflect, often with microscopic accuracy, the mood of the nation'.[15] Theatre of this kind reflects and presents issues within a nation but also focuses on trying to change them. *Posh*'s perceived impact on dining societies at Oxford University is one example of how a play can both describe a social phenomenon and also change it.

Alex Sierz described new writing such as this as 'an ongoing conversation, often a debate, sometimes a polemic, about who we are and what we might become'.[16] In doing so, he highlights the stylistic diversity that is contained within this genre. Élisabeth Angel-Perez explores this concept further. For her, realism and satire often combine in the state of the nation play:

> Ever since the Bard [Shakespeare]'s celebration of
> desecrated national icons (Richard III, Richard II, Lear,
> Macbeth), England has been the country of satire, a country
> in which the nation builds itself against the nation [. . .]. Such
> plays belong either to the socio-realistic approach or/and to
> the satirical or more openly political[17]

The style, content and impact of *Posh* all suggest a State of the Nation play but the most compelling evidence can be seen in the development of the play text between its first run at the Royal Court in 2010, which took place under a Labour Government, and the West End run (printed in this edition) performed during the Conservative/Liberal Democrat coalition government in 2012.

The major difference between the versions can be found at the beginning of Act Two. In 2010, much of the conversation about the current situation in the UK is focussed on how the Riot Club's social class is a hindrance to their role in potentially occupying positions of power. In 2012, this exchange is modified to incorporate the shift in UK politics which involved the Eton and Oxford-educated David Cameron becoming Prime Minister. By comparing the exchange in

---

[15] Michael Billington. 'Lifting the Curtain'. *The Guardian*. 24 October 2007.

[16] Aleks Sierz. *Rewriting the Nation.* London: Bloomsbury Methuen Drama, 2011. p. 225.

[17] Élisabeth Angel-Perez. 'Deconstructing the nation? British Theatre in the Age of Postmodernism'. Hopes, Jeffrey, and Héléne Lecossois. *Théâtre et nation*. Rennes: Presses universitaires de Rennes, 2011. p. 62.

2010 to the passage between pages 93–94 in this edition, one can see Wade updating the text to reflect the state of the nation:

2010 Text

George   Our roof's got holes you could fire a cow through.

Dimitri   Bored of the roof now!

Alistair   It's not your fault you can't see it, mate. People get used to being shat on, don't they? I mean when did we get so timid? Why are we sneaking around pretending we're the Young Farmers? We are being oppressed.

James   Oh come on, for fuck's sake –

Alistair   Seriously, mate.

George   Why's everyone being so –

Alistair   What?

George   Hate it when there's fighting. Drink up and be mates.

Alistair   The world doesn't like us.

Guy   They hate us.[18]

2012 Text

George   Our roof's got holes you could fire a cow through.

Dimitri   Bored of the roof now!

James   I'm just saying your family benefited from –

Harry   Yeah, till they stopped coming.

Alistair   And we know why they stopped, don't we? Cause they spent all the money on all this shiny new shit – massive fuckoff plasma-screen telly. Don't understand why they're not just born with it, why it doesn't just get handed to them –

James   OK, sure, 'mistakes were made', but our lot us are in power now, so –

Guy   True dat.

Alistair   We're not in power.

Guy   They'll get a majority next time, my uncle says

---

[18]   Laura Wade. *Posh*. London: Oberon Books, 2010.

The 'us versus them' attitude of the Riot Club and their perceived victimhood, despite their privilege, is prevalent in both editions. However, Wade ensures the nuance of the social situation in the United Kingdom at the time of writing is established. In doing so she satirises an existing facet of British social and political life within a realistic setting.

Play as performance

As the professional performance history of *Posh* demonstrates, the play offers a multitude of possibilities for actors and members of creative teams. Counting the original production of *Posh* at the Royal Court and its West End run in 2012 as separate entities, as of February 2023, there have been five different professional productions of *Posh* in the UK – all of which are explored in the following section and the next to provide inspiration for future work. Following 2012, a new staging of the Wade's play was presented at the Nottingham Playhouse and Salisbury Playhouse in 2015, an all-female cast performed the play in 2017, and the most recent incarnation of *Posh* was staged at the Oxford Playhouse in 2019.

Casting

In his five star review of the 2017 all-female production of *Posh*, the *Independent*'s chief theatre critic, Paul Taylor, suggested that it 'should be performed like this from now on'.[19] Cressida Carré's production was received as a biting satire, utilizing more heightened performances that, according to Taylor, 'slips the last surly bonds of "realism"'.[20] In contrast to this, the 2010 production (which cast the roles within the written genders) was often praised for the convincing, realistic portrayal of character, particularly in Wade's use of language. Tim Auld writing in the traditionally Conservative *Sunday*

---

[19]   Paul Taylor. 'Posh, Pleasure Theatre: Review'. *The Independent*. 4 April 2017.
[20]   Ibid.

Telegraph suggested that, 'Wade, a comprehensive school girl from Sheffield, has pulled off an extraordinary feat of ventriloquism. There is nothing parodic about the dialogue; she writes – and I confess some insider knowledge here – as public schoolboys speak when they meet as a pack'.[21]

The response to these productions highlights the stylistic versatility of the text in *Posh* and how casting decisions can be used to sharpen whatever satirical edge a creative team wants to bring out in the play. Wade is supportive of different casting approaches.

Behind the scenes

Laura Wade: I'm all for people of all genders taking on the parts. To inhabit those characters is a really useful way of understanding the play. I think this play is much more about class than it is about gender. When I've seen women take on those roles, the ones that have worked best have not been about accurately portraying a man as much as being able to embody the entitlement, the swagger and the ease that those boys need to have. That's worth thinking about when playing them rather than whether or not you're being a convincing boy.

Each production can create its own rules and I think it is there to be played with. It's important to me that it is a group of men being represented, I don't think a group of women behaves in the same way. In the course of our research we talked to somebody who was from a female dining society – they didn't go round smashing up pubs. It's quite a different thing. While it's not only about masculinity, god knows there are enough plays about that, I think it is a group of men. But, whatever, go for it – the play is there to be explored.

---

21   Tim Auld. Rev. of Posh, dir. Lyndsey Turner. *Sunday Telegraph* 25 April 2010.

Stage and lighting design

On the surface, *Posh* offers a straightforward task for a stage designer. There are two locations which are clearly described by Wade (5, 14) in a simple fashion which leaves plenty of room for interpretation. The stage design, however, is a key factor in establishing the level of realism the production is adopting.

Attitude to space is formed from an early age so researching the schools in which the Riot Club were educated can be useful for those designing *Posh*. Writer, poet and podcaster, Musa Okwonga attended Eton in the 1990s and published *One of Them: An Eton Memoir* (2021), which documents his time there from a personal perspective. In Okwonga's view, the school's buildings are key to evoking an attitude in its pupils: 'No one here ever tells us out loud that we Etonians are natural leaders: that is what the architecture is for'.[22] The disregard with which the Riot Club treats the Bull's Head in the play comes from a childhood spent around very different buildings to that of the gastropub. Eton pupils take exams, read books and attend concerts in imposing and impressive buildings which boast domes, arches and classical columns. Alistair's anger, revealed at the end of Act One, is an outburst from someone accustomed to such architectural opulence being forced, instead, to spend time in more mundane surrounds:

> I mean who the fuck does he – Does he think he's some kind of lord cause he's got a gastropub? What, thin beef and gay puddings for people who think cause they're eating orange fish it must be smoked salmon?
>
> (89)

The reviews of the original production in 2010 rarely mention Anthony Ward's design, but Susannah Clapp, writing for *The Observer*, noticed that it: 'shows a pub dining room hung with antlers and landscapes, striving for draughty country house grandeur'.[23] This could be an important area of exploration for those

---

22   Musa Okwonga. *One Of Them: An Eton College Memoir*. London: Unbound, 2021. p. 27.
23   Susannah Clapp. Rev. of Posh, dir. Lyndsey Turner. *The Observer* 18 April 2010.

staging the play – to what degree is the setting for the Riot Club's meeting an 'Ikea version' of the stately homes which the characters discuss at the beginning of Act Two? The environment fuels the frustration at their perceived fall from grace. Lighting is also vital to this, and contrasting the lighting states in the two locations can speak to a key theme of the play. Often simple practical lighting decisions can mark the difference between an exclusive, private environment to the more every day location of a gastropub.

The latent anger contained within many of The Riot Club, comes to a head in the narrative climax of the play: the trashing of The Bull's Head. Wade's decision to stage the vandalism feels deliberate and serves to counter any sympathy that might have built-up between the characters and the audience. Their entitlement becomes violent and it is any designer's job working on *Posh* to create a set which is both breakable but also capable of being reassembled for the next performance. Wade has some advice for those adopting these creative roles:

Behind the scenes

Laura Wade: It's probably important for the director and designer to talk very early in the design process about the practical considerations of the trashing, because the set needs to have 'trashability' built into it from the start.

For maximum impact, the trashing needs to be as visually impressive as it can possibly be: if you imagine you've spent the whole play up to this point building a bomb, then this is the moment the bomb explodes. For the audience it's a shocking inevitability. For the boys, it's their catharsis, a release of a lot of pent-up anger. But also in a weird way, there's joy because they delight in a job well done, a room well trashed.

Like everything that outwardly looks chaotic, it needs to be forensically choreographed. And it needs to take a while, because if it's too quick you feel short-changed.

So what's the maximum mess you can make and still clear up in time for the next performance (particularly on days when

---

there's a matinee and an evening show)? What can you hide around the set that can be pulled out and scattered? You've also got to make it safe: the Riot Club might love the sound of breaking glass, but your stage manager almost certainly won't.

The all-female production of 2017 drew more focus to the satirical aspect of the play and the stage design played a crucial part in its political message. Paul Taylor, writing in *The Independent*, observed 'The accoutrements of privilege are surrounded by stark, gutted walls in Sara Perks' powerfully suggestive design. It's as if the horror is always a foregone conclusion on these occasions'.[24] Perks' design used a stripped back aesthetic to establish a foreboding mood, and opened space for the female cast to satirise the behaviour of the Riot Club with a more exaggerated performance style.

Costume design

The 1987 Bullingdon Club photograph presented the group in formal dress coats, highlighting their class and their separation from mainstream society. For Okwonga, the power of clothing is a fundamental aspect of the breeding of a privileged attitude, something he himself experienced as an Eton pupil:

The greatest proof of my status [...] Every single day I go to class in clothing that many men wear only once in their lives, if at all: a morning suit, identical to the clothing of a bridegroom [...] The effect of this is that, when I put on a business suit for work or any formal occasion, I look as relaxed as if I am wearing a pair of pyjamas.[25]

Wade chooses to have the Riot Club in a specific uniform, and draws attention to its importance early in the play. Harry's main focus when arriving is to find a space to get dressed properly: 'I'm not putting my tails on in the loo, fuck's sake' (19). The connection between the behaviour and material conditions of the characters, such as costume,

---

[24]   Paul Taylor. 'Posh, Pleasure Theatre: Review'. *The Independent*. 4 April 2017.

[25]   Musa Okwonga. *One Of Them: An Eton College Memoir*. London: Unbound, 2021 p. 32.

is a key focus for any director and designer of the play. In the 2010 production, one privately schooled, Oxford-educated critic took issue with the costume: 'no visitor to the kind of high-Tory London club that frames the action would be admitted without a tie'.[26]

Sound design and music

A cursory look through *Posh* would not necessarily lead a reader to see the vivid potential of sound design and music in performance. The production history of the play can, however, inspire those seeking to explore these aspects of the stage aesthetic. In the 2010 and 2012 stagings, the scene changes were striking and added complexity to the performance.

Behind the scenes

Laura Wade: In the original production, the scene changes used an a-cappella vocal group style that we were aware of existing at Oxford University with groups like Out of the Blue. Three mornings a week we'd start the rehearsal day with a singing session with [the composer] James Fortune and the other two days, they'd have a fencing lesson. It was all part of the 'posh-boot-camp' which brought everybody up to speed. I think the singing in the scene changes worked, as Lyndsey Turner [the director] had intended it to, because it reset the 'charm dial' and the audience would enjoy the laugh of recognition when they recognised the song, it gave a little pop of joy between scenes, which offset some of their less positive feelings towards the characters. The actors did it really well, we had some really good singers in that group. Also, the songs had a thematic relevance like 'Earthquake' by Labrinth that has lyrics like 'We're on a rampage/ bottles poppin' off/Before you know it, there's rubble and dust/'Cause we'll be fuckin' it up'.

---

26   Michael Billington. Rev. of *Posh*, dir. Lyndsey Turner. *Guardian*. 16 April 2010.

Subsequent productions have also used music in scene changes to challenge audiences' perception of the characters. Susannah Tresilian's 2015 production at the Nottingham Playhouse impressed a visiting critic, who noted, 'whereas the original production featured close harmony vocal arrangements in the breaks between scenes, Tresilian employs an accomplished soprano, Joanne Evans, to provide classy operatic entr'actes in addition to her less classy interaction as the call girl employed to perform blow jobs under the table'. [27] Isobel Waller-Bridge's work with music and sound for this production gave a subtle reminder of the dismissive attitude that the Riot Club have for those outside of their immediate experience.

Staging

Most of the performance takes place with the ten-strong group on stage which requires close scrutiny of the shifts in status, and internal and external thought processes.

Behind the scenes

Laura Wade: Lyndsey Turner was very good at pulling me up on the fact we were creating ten people and we needed to find ways to make sure they're all different. We were examining ten subspecies that all have their own very specific kind of personality. George is very country-posh and has a different background to Alistair who is much more urban-posh. Miles is more urban still, he's a Notting-Hill-West-London-posh. Dmitri is from a 'Euro-money' background and doesn't have the 'class' but has the cash. At some point we made Top Trumps cards for all of them: How much money do they have, how much 'class status' do they have, what's their charm, how much anger do they have – all these different kinds of things that you could work out for each of them.

---

[27]   Alfred Hickling. Rev. of *Posh*, dir. Susannah Tresilian. *Guardian*. 23 February 2015.

To use an example, homophobic language is integrated into many of the interactions of the Riot Club, a fact even more disturbing if one considers that Hugo is gay (79). Performers playing members of the Riot Club could, therefore, strongly consider their internal monologue when prejudiced behaviours occur in front of them unchallenged. What is holding them back from confronting it? The detail of these decisions can play an important part in the movement, or lack of it, on stage during the performance. When this detail is not explored entirely, critics have complained: A review of the 2019 Oxford Playhouse production, for example, noted that the 'characters rather blend together into a single boozed-up, braying mob. A pity because Wade's writing glitters. Her play is as evisceratingly savage as ever; this production, though, is terribly tame'.[28]

Behind the scenes

Laura Wade: Try to slow it down in rehearsal and work out who is talking to who around the table. There's points when there are several conversations ping-ponging around the table. Slow all of that down before you speed it up. If you hit it at too much of a lick [speed] straight away you can get yourself in a tangle. You need to rehearse it with pinpoint accuracy so that on stage it can look chaotic.

We thought a lot in rehearsals that to the boys, it's more important to win the argument than believe the thing you are talking about. Years after the play was written, it's absolutely what Boris did with his two Brexit columns in the Daily Telegraph. It was Debate Society for him, an afternoon in the [Oxford] Union.

Production history and critical reception

Posh premiered in 2010 at the Royal Court Theatre in London, directed by Lyndsey Turner. Situated on Sloane Square on the King's

---

[28]   Sam Marlowe. Rev. of *Posh*, dir. Lucy Hughes. *The Times*. 10 September 2019.

Road, the Royal Court is in one of the wealthiest parts of London but is also the highest-profile New Writing theatre in the UK. This nuanced identity is important to consider alongside the critical reception of the play: to what extent did the original production of *Posh* function as a piece of political theatre? Or, was the production holding up a mirror to a section of the Royal Court audience who occupy and maintain positions of power? It is also important to acknowledge that many of the professional theatre critics who were reviewing the production were white, male, privately educated Oxford graduates or former Oxford University employees.

Michael Billington (St Catherine's College, Oxford), who wrote a three-star review in *The Guardian*, questioned the authenticity of the violent climax of the play since, 'even within the ranks of the bluebloods, there were occasional spasms of doubt and decency'.[29] Paul Taylor of *The Independent* (Balliol College, Oxford) found Charlie's competence in discoursing with the Riot Club hard to believe, suggesting that 'It's the aplomb with which she does so that sounds false'.[30] Like Billington, Taylor criticized Wade's portrayal of the Riot Club as lacking another side to their behaviour, 'we never see any of these young men except through the lens of their Riot Club membership'.

The review in the *Daily Mail*, a right-wing tabloid newspaper, reflected the political compass of former boarding school pupil and Cambridge University graduate, Quentin Letts. While the technical elements of Wade's writing were praised in Letts' three-star write up, he described the play as a 'political attack' using language and epithets that seem strikingly similar to the Riot Club's: 'Were Miss Wade better informed, she might write about the unreconstructed, male-dominated power nexus of the trade unions and the Labour party'.[31] Aleks Sierz (University of Manchester), writing for the ArtsDesk website, saw *Posh* as a State of the Nation Play: 'this play feels like a key cultural moment that seems to accurately take the temperature of the times'.[32] This range of critical responses reflects

[29]   Michael Billington. 'Posh' *Guardian*. 16 April 2010.
[30]   Paul Taylor. 'Posh, Royal Court Theatre, London' *Independent*. 19 April 2010.
[31]   Quentin Letts. 'It's toffs at the top in this classy satire'. *Daily Mail*. 16 April 2010.
[32]   Aleks Sierz. 'Posh, Review'. *The Arts Desk*. 15 April 2010.

the deep-rooted influence of elite institutions like Oxford University in British cultural life.

Two years after the original production, *Posh* transferred to the Duke of York's Theatre in London's West End. The creative team was retained (aside from the lighting designer) and Wade rewrote parts of the script. Billington suggested that the changes in the script improved the production: 'On a second viewing, it becomes clear that Wade's chief target is not just privileged toffs but the cosy network that really runs Britain'.[33] Taylor also remarked how the revisions reflected the rise of the Conservative Party in the intervening two-year period between productions and improved the script. Despite this, he continued to present his view of the play as 'One-sided in its sympathies'.[34] Writing for *The Arts Desk*, Carmel Doohan (Nottingham University) drew attention to the links between female representation and the political position of the play: 'The play which is written and directed by women locates in its female characters the new world the boys fear, a world which neither respects nor needs them'.[35]

The 2017 all-female production, directed by Cressida Carré at the Pleasance Theatre, London, developed these ideas in even more detail. As previously mentioned, Taylor's position on *Posh* changed once he had seen the play staged in this way. In the hands of Carré, *Posh* became a 'Biting, grotesque fable about a class that wants to reassert its brutal rights to special treatment – with the exhilarating twist that the oppressors are played by a group traditionally perceived as oppressed'.[36] Corrie Tan (Brown University, US), writing for *The Guardian*, praised the cast's performances who were 'clearly exaggerating their characters' masculine traits'.[37] Aside from qualitative judgements about the production, this 2017 staging clearly had an impact on the play's critical reception and highlights the stylistic versatility that is at the core of the text.

[33] Michael Billington. '*Posh* – Review'. *Guardian*. 23 May 2012.
[34] Paul Taylor. 'First Night: *Posh*, Duke of York's Theatre, London'. *Independent*. 23 May 2012.
[35] Carmel Doohan. '*Posh*, Duke of York's Theatre: Review'. *The Arts Desk*. 24 May 2012.
[36] Paul Taylor. '*Posh*, Pleasure Theatre: Review'. *The Independent*. 4 April 2017.
[37] Corrie Tan. '*Posh* review – Laura Wade's Bullingdon boys become lairy ladies who lunch'. *Guardian*. 4 April 2017.

Behind the scenes

Laura Wade: I was really impressed with the all-female production. It was the most accurate line learn I'd ever seen of the play. I wanted to get a T-Shirt made with 'Girls Do It Properly'. They were 100 per cent on the lines. For me, that's when I can hear the play. Sometimes when people are learning the play, they don't trust the lines to do the work for them. It's a sweary, fuck-y play – and sometimes people think that if they add in a few extra fucks it'll make it better but actually it can make it feel baggy and unfocused. If the script can be followed like a musical score and trusted, it works best.

Further exploration

Elaine Aston. 'Structure of Class Feeling/Feeling of Class Structure: Laura Wade's *Posh* and Katherine Soper's *Wish List*'. *Modern Drama*, 61(2). Toronto: University of Toronto Press, 2018 (pp. 127–48)

Dan Rebellato. *Playwrights in Lockdown: Laura Wade*. YouTube. 24 April 2020

Laura Wade. *Plays One*. London: Bloomsbury Methuen Drama, 2021.[38]

---

[38] Aleks Sierz's Introduction to this text provides detailed contextual analysis of Wade's writing and how it functions in performance.

Posh

For Lyndsey

Posh grew out of a close writer-director collaboration initiated by the Royal Court *Rough Cuts* programme. We'd like to thank the following people and organisations who helped with the development of the play:

Sebastian Armesto, Diane Borger, Fiona Button, Pandora Colin, Jamie Doyle, Julia Gibson, Heather Hooper, Rory Kinnear, Charlotte Knight, Harry Lloyd, Out of the Blue, Oxford University Dramatic Society, William Russell, Rafe Spall, Samuel West, Timothy West, Will Woodward, Victoria Yeates, Peter York, John Bashford and the students of LAMDA, and all of the actors who contributed at various stages of work on the script.

Also Ari Edelson and all at the Orchard Project and Catskill Mountains Foundation, the staff and supporters of *Rough Cuts*, Ruth Little, Dominic Cooke, Jeremy Herrin and all at the Royal Court Theatre, in particular Emily McLaughlin, who championed the project from the start.

Characters

The Riot Club:

Guy Bellingfield
James Leighton-Masters
Toby Maitland
George Balfour
Alistair Ryle
Hugo Fraser-Tyrwhitt
Harry Villiers
Miles Richards
Dimitri Mitropoulos
Ed Montgomery

Plus:

Jeremy, *Guy's godfather*
Chris, *the landlord of The Bull's Head*
Rachel, *Chris' daughter*
Charlie, *an escort*

Act One

Scene One

A Gentlemen's Club in London. A wood-panelled room with two big leather armchairs and a small table between them.

Jeremy *sits in one of the chairs, sipping from a glass of whisky.* **Guy** *stands opposite him.*

Jeremy   Don't stand there like a schoolboy, Guy – take a seat.

Guy   That a new chap on the desk?

Jeremy   They're all bloody new.

Guy   Told me you were upstairs in the Blue Room.

Jeremy   Idiot.

Guy   I said concentrate, mate – I'm not even a member and even I know the Blue Room's the one downstairs,

Jeremy   Which isn't actually blue.

Guy   Which isn't actually blue. The one you're talking about, despite having blue walls, I said, is actually the Oak Room.

Jeremy   Bloody foreign staff. Still, they can book you a cab in seven languages.

Guy   So. How's the mood in the camp?

Jeremy   Oh, you know.

Guy   Amazing, yeah – feet under the table, back in the saddle, ducks in a row, heads above parapets,

Jeremy   Too many metaphors.

Guy   Just the table one, then.

Jeremy   Standing there with a dustpan and brush in your hand, clearing up after someone else's party.

Guy   No, yeah, course. I mean, what, 13 years on the sidelines? Long winter.

Jeremy   Hard to make people love you when it's all cut cut cut.

Guy   No, sure.

Jeremy   Just set up a group to work on Operation Charm Offensive.

Guy   Excellent.

Jeremy   All they've dreamed up so far is a monthly backbenchers' Curry Night.

Guy   Poppadoms and policy.

Jeremy   Men of the people, you know.

Guy   And women.

Jeremy   People of the people. More offensive than charming, so far.

How's college?

Guy   Yeah good good.

Jeremy   Playing any Rugger?

Guy   Only when they're desperate.

Jeremy   Your mother tells me you're seeing some girl.

Guy   Well. Yeah. I mean it's not –

Jeremy   Bit out of the loop, aren't I?

Guy   Yeah, it's been a while.

Jeremy   Bit remiss with the godfathering?

Guy   No, god no. I mean I totally know you're here when I need you, so –

Guy *pauses.*

Jeremy   Drink?

Guy   Yes please.

Jeremy *pours two tumblers of whisky.*

Jeremy   Water?

Guy   Ice please.

Jeremy *looks at* **Guy***: wrong answer. He puts some ice into* **Guy***'s drink.*

Jeremy   So what's her name?

Guy   Lauren.

Jeremy   *Lauren.*

D'you know, I don't know a single person called *Lauren* isn't that remarkable?

Guy   Not really.

Jeremy   Lauren what, Lauren who?

Guy   Lauren Small.

Jeremy   Small. Is she?

Guy   Not where it matters.

Jeremy   Where's she from?

Guy   Hastings.

Jeremy   Charming. And the parents?

Guy   They have a chain of shops.

Jeremy   Selling what?

Guy   Magazines, newspapers.

Jeremy   A newsagent?

Guy   Chain of them. Several.

Jeremy   Cigarettes and chocolate. Well, people always popping out for a pint of milk. Or *scratch cards*.

Guy   Language.

Jeremy   Where'd she go to school?

Guy   In Hastings.

Jeremy   Day school?

Guy   Comprehensive.

Jeremy   Clever girl, getting to Oxford.

Guy   First in the family.

Jeremy   Goes like the clappers as well, I expect.

Guy *sips his drink.*

In case it helps, Guy, I'm liable to be called back to the Lords any moment, so if you've something to ask, I'd spit it out.

Guy   Right, no, of course. You're very busy.

OK, right.

It's the – It's the Riot Club. We're back in business. This term.

Jeremy   Yes, I thought it might be that.

Guy   You knew, did you?

Jeremy   Yes.

Guy   James had a call from – James Leighton-Masters, the president –

Jeremy   Yes, I know.

Guy   Had a call from another old member –

Jeremy   Michael Bingham, yes I know.

Guy   Said it's been long enough since –

Jeremy   Yes.

Guy   OK, then you know all of it.

Jeremy   No, please – Go on.

Guy   OK, so we're back, we can start having dinners again, Embargo Relaxum.

Jeremy   On the proviso that you keep it out of the Daily Mail this time, right?

Guy   Well yeah.

Yeah, but that wasn't about a dinner, though, was it, that story, that was just Toby –

Jeremy   You know what I mean.

Guy   I know we've missed two dinners because of him knobbing about. And you don't get very many, do you, one a term? Not many chances to –

Jeremy   To let rip.

Guy   To make your mark.

If you want to be the next president.

Jeremy   Oh, Guy –

Guy   Elections after Christmas, so –

Jeremy   Why d'you want the hassle of being president?

Guy   You know, for the old CV.

Jeremy   Current climate, Guy – employers don't like –

Guy   Not my written CV, obviously. I mean the curriculum of my *actual* vitae.

The legend of Guy Bellingfield.

So I was thinking I could bring something special to the next dinner. Sort of a trailer. As well as, you know, celebrating the. Glorious return.

And, I just, I know that back in the day, you were – you know, you were quite a legend in the club.

Jeremy   Right.

Guy   And I'm a bit, um. Stuck for ideas.

Jeremy   I think you're over-thinking it.

Guy   Just want a bit of inspiration.

Jeremy   It's only a club.

Guy   It's the best club.

Jeremy   Silly student japes, all it is. Letting off steam.

Guy   Please, just. Anything. Please.

Jeremy   Alright, well. Why don't you pitch in with club finances? – chap did that when I was at college, managed the funds judiciously enough to lay down a cellar of really excellent wine for future dinners, that showed a bit of foresight –

Guy   Yeah, I was thinking of something that might have a bit more of an um, immediate impact. Something with a bit of, you know. Woof.

Jeremy   You know the best thing you could do, Guy, for your *CV*, is ensure this dinner passes pretty uneventfully.

Guy   Right.

Jeremy   Yes?

Guy   Yeah, sorry, OK. Uneventful. Lead by example. The Quiet Man.

Jeremy   Exactly.

Guy   Just easy to get carried away when I grew up on all those stories. Listening to you talk about the club, all the amazing – obviously, that was before things were so –

Jeremy   Sadly, yes.

Guy   God, that one about the – was it a chandelier?

Jeremy   I don't –

Guy   Yeah no, you and the guys – massive food fight, something about a chandelier got caught in the crossfire, shattered everywhere –

Jeremy   One chandelier was hardly a rare occurrence in those days.

Guy   No, yeah, not just *one* –

Jeremy   Christ, some dinners there'd be three chandeliers broken before we even sat down –

Guy   Amazing.

Jeremy   We'd be eating in the dark sometimes.

Guy   Legends.

Jeremy   You know one time – this was bloody funny – we stripped a dining room *totally* bare – wallpaper down, floorboards up –

Of course we were all, you know,

Guy   Three sheets to the wind.

Jeremy   More than that.

Guy   Four sheets to the wind.

Jeremy   Took all the electrics out, skirting boards, dado rails, put it all in a huge pile in the middle of the floor –

Guy   Sounds amazing.

Jeremy   Work of genius. Should have seen the owner's face when he saw it.

Guy   Did he go ballistic?

Jeremy   Once we'd given him a blank cheque he thought it was bloody funny, actually. Very nice chap, gave us a lift to the station. Not quite sure how we got there but the next morning we woke up in Vienna.

Guy   Vienna?

Jeremy   Passed out face down in a box of marzipan.

Guy   Wow. Did you always go somewhere?

Jeremy   After dinner, yes. A jaunt.

Guy   That's it – I should totally arrange a trip – cause we usually just end up in a club – I mean wow, this could be seriously –

Jeremy   But I thought you weren't going to –

Guy   Val d'Isere, maybe – bit of drunken skiing –

Jeremy   *Uneventful* we said –

Guy   Or maybe just taxis to the airport – just rock up and take a chance on the next flight out. Have Gold Card, Will Travel. How presidential is that? The Riot Club hits Heathrow.

Jeremy   No, Guy, Guy, wait, think –

Guy   What?

Jeremy   Think about the *dinner*. If you're going to do something.

Guy   What?

Jeremy   Surely what – what happens *inside* the room. Much more important than where you go afterwards. If you're set on leading by example. If you want to make your mark as a leader, not just a, you know, *holiday rep*.

Guy   So . . .

Jeremy   Well, it's the dinner *itself* – you know, give it some grandeur, some *meaning*. The wine, for example – put some real thought into it: the perfect complement to the ten-bird roast, the perfect Sauternes for the pudding, the –

Guy   Complement to the what?

Jeremy   Pudding.

Guy   No, before that, you said –

Jeremy   Ten-bird roast.

Guy   What's a ten-bird roast?

Jeremy   What it says, isn't it, a bird inside a bird inside a bird and so on.

Guy   Ten different birds.

Because there's ten of us in the club, see.

Jeremy   Oh now, there, I'd forgotten.

Guy   Like a metaphor, for – What sort of birds is it?

Jeremy   I don't know, quail, duck, partridge, whatever, you don't cook it yourself I don't know exactly what's in it.

But bloody special. I mean this is you connecting yourself to hundreds of years of history.

Guy   A sacrament, almost.

Jeremy   Exactly that – a sacrament. Ten of you, bound together –

Guy   Brotherhood again.

Jeremy   Exactly. Bonding over the meat and the fire.

Guy   And you definitely think that'll work –

Jeremy   It's what they had at the first ever dinner.

Guy   Savage, OK.

So maybe James'd let me take charge of the whole menu – say I'm just trying to help him out – get something properly impressive like a ten bird roast –

Jeremy   Show you're a man of taste and discernment.

Guy   Awesome president material.

Jeremy   There you go. There's your game plan.

Guy   And then we tear the place apart later.

Jeremy   Guy –

Guy   Jokes, Uncle Jezza – I'm joking.

Jeremy*'s phone chimes.*

Jeremy   Oh god, here we go –

He holds his phone up to show **Guy**.

There's an app now, for the Division Bell.

Guy   Nice.

Jeremy   Look, I – I can't stress enough how important it is that you –

If you can be an arbiter of sense and decorum at that dinner, you'll make me, and others in more elevated positions extremely –

Guy   Don't worry. We'll be good boys, we won't disappoint.

Jeremy   You know what I mean. No fucking about, yes?

Jeremy*'s phone chimes again.*

Guy   Thanks, Uncle Jezza.

Jeremy *leaves.*

Guy *leans back in his chair, looks around the room.*

Guy*'s phone rings. He picks up.*

Dimitri, you massive gayer! Listen to this: it's going to be fucking *savage*.

Blackout.

Scene Two

The private dining room at the Bull's Head Inn, set for dinner, but empty at first. **Chris** *and* **George** *enter.* **George** *looks around, surprised that the room is empty.*

Chris   You're the first.

George   Yeah. Savage.

Chris   Well you can tell me if everything's OK – anything you think you'll need you can't see here?

George   Uh. Yeah. I'm not really the –

Not really the right chap.

Chris   Been to a wedding?

George   Uh, no, it's uh. Club regimentals.

I mean it's –

Chris   Thought you'd be in business suits, more of a pinstripe thing.

George   Sorry?

Chris   Young Entrepreneurs.

George   Oh yes, yeah. Young Entrepreneurs Club.

Chris   I thought that'd be, you know. Entrepreneurs *now*.

George   Yeah, it's uh. It's retro night. Lovely.

Chris   Well, take a pew, make yourself at home.

George *looks at a chair, then looks around the room, at a loss.*

George   Yeah, bit weird. On my own. Might go and sit out –

Chris   Whatever you prefer.

Chris *ushers* **George** *out of the door.*

George   Have you got a snug?

The room is left empty.

Moments later, the door opens again and **Toby** *comes in, seething and full of nervy energy.* **Ed** *follows behind.* **Toby** *is carrying a vintage-looking leather box with a handle – looks like a hat box – and an ornamental sabre in a velvet pouch attached to a sash.*

Ed   Mate, I'm sorry, OK.

Toby   You're not supposed to move your stuff, fuck's sake.

Ed   Is this what you were pissed off about in the cab? You could have said –

Toby   Looked like Soviet Russia. Like a monk who's taken a vow of no fucking possessions.

Ed   Just my computer and the stereo.

Toby   What, nothing else?

Little furry friend?

Ed   Yeah, OK.

Toby   Mr Ted, Big Ted, whatever its name is.

Ed   It's just that my brother said –

Toby   He told you to move your stuff out?

Ed   No, he just. Mentioned there'd be something and I knew it'd be either a bedroom-trash or a beasting cause it always is, so – Pre-emptive strike.

Toby   Fucking weasel.

Supposed to be awesome. Your entry to the club. They knew soon as they walked in and couldn't find Mr Fucking Snuffles.

Ed   Kingsley. Kingsley Bear.

Toby   Walk in and it's 'where's the bear? Hmm, *nowhere'*.

Ed   I'm sorry, mate.

Toby   I'm your sponsor. You fuck it up, it reflects back on me.

Ed   Yeah, sorry.

Toby   Stop saying fucking sorry. Just. Try not to make me look like a twat.

Ed *sits down.*

Mate!

Ed   What?

Ed *jumps up.*

Toby   You don't sit before the president.

Ed   Yeah, I know, I just thought. He's not here yet. No one's here.

Toby   Dinner starts when you walk through that door. Jesus.

Toby *paces, hands in pockets.*

Where the fuck are they?

Ed   Long way to come, isn't it, cause of the, um – Radius –

Ed *looks at* **Toby** *– he doesn't yet seem appeased.*

Toby, I'm sorry about the bear, OK? He's a family heirloom.

Toby   '*He*'?

Ed   Kingsley Bear has been in my family for like, three generations, a hundred years. If anything happens to him – *it* – I mean my grandmother would go ballistic and she's scary –

Toby   Why d'you bring it to college?

Ed   Family tradition.

Toby   Fuck's sake.

Ed   Look, mate, I get it.

Toby   What?

Ed   I know you've got a rep to repair. I know you're worried the guys are still hacked off at you for the Daily Mail thing, but we've all done stupid shit, yeah? And I know you didn't want to be my sponsor, but I'm going to be distressingly awesome tonight. Team Tubes.

Toby   Mate, fuck, look, tonight's a write off – they're going to tear me a new one, give me a fucking dregsing, and I'm going to put my head down and take it cause once they've done that they can't say anything.

But I don't need you cocking about in my eyeline, making it worse, ok? I'm on thin ice here.

Ed   Toby, I'm your skates.

Toby   What?

Harry (*off*)   This one through here? No no, I'll be fine, thank you so much.

Ed   Skates, like ice skates –

Toby   Just stay out my way.

The door opens and **Harry** *comes in backwards, rather overloaded. He's wearing full fencing gear and carries a large kit bag, with a couple of swords sticking out of it, plus a suit carrier.*

Harry   Yeah yeah, I can manage I'll just whack it in a corner.

Ooh, hello. Private moment?

Toby   No-one's here yet.

Ed   Hi Harry.

Toby *goes into the hat box and takes out a white powdered 1760s-style wig, which he puts on his head during the next.*

Harry   Cut the air with a knife.

Ed   Or a sword.

Harry   Oh, it does jokes. (*To* **Toby**.) Well picked.

Toby   Didn't pick him.

Harry *hands his kit bag to* **Ed**.

Harry   Ed?

Harry *unzips his suit carrier and takes out his tails.* **Toby** *puts on the sash and ornamental sword.* **Harry** *notices.*

Wig of shame, nice.

Toby   You've had a match?

Harry   1 had a match – other chap had a pasting.

Toby   Varsity?

Harry   Varsity warm-up. They haven't got a chance.

Ed   You won then?

Harry   I always win.

Pasted the captain and then got a blowjob off his girlfriend while he was getting looked at by the physio.

Ed   Fuck.

Harry   Tab shoo!

Toby   Was she fit?

Harry   She was from Cambridge. Still, blowjob's a blowjob.

Right, can you fuck off for a minute while I get changed?

Toby   In here?

Harry   Yeah.

Toby   Why didn't you dress at college?

Harry   No time – two hours ago I was still in the rotten Fens. Got dropped off by the minibus.

Toby   Whyn't you change in the loo?

Harry   I'm not putting my tails on in the loo, fuck's sake. Just go out in the bar a minute.

Toby   I'm not going out there.

Ed   Toby got wolf-whistled on the way in.

Harry   So the locals think you're hot.

Toby   Stand around like a twat when we can't even have a drink yet.

Chris *comes in.*

Chris   Everything alright, gents?

Harry   Excellent, thank you.

Chris   Just looking for James Leighton-Masters.

Toby   He's not here yet.

Harry   Leighton's not here yet?

Chris   Look like a musketeer.

Toby   Charades later.

Toby *takes off the sash and sword and leans it against the wall.*

Chris   Alright, well – If he comes in could you point him towards me?

Toby   Absolutely.

Chris *goes to leave.*

Harry   Hi – sorry – actually I could do with a bit of a brush-down. Have you got a room?

Chris   A room?

Harry   You do bed and breakfast, right?

Chris   'Restaurant with Rooms', yes.

Harry   Yes, of course – very good. Could I possibly *borrow* a room – just for half an hour? Don't fancy changing in the loo, you know?

Chris   Thing is we're full tonight – you know, Saturday – they're all booked.

Harry   Oh boo – I mean great, obviously. Are they all here?

Chris   Pardon?

Harry   Have they all arrived, are the rooms actually occupied right now?

Chris   Not yet, no.

Harry   Just if I could possibly pop into one for like, half an hour. Less than.

Chris   Thing is, the rooms have got to be ready when they come, so –

Harry   No no, sure sure. I'm talking about paying, by the way. I mean how much does a room go for? Per night.

Chris   Eighty five pounds.

Harry   Gosh that's reasonable.

Ed   So for half an hour that's what, eighty five divided by twenty-four –

Harry   Eighty-five, full whack.

Chris   For half an hour?

Harry   You'd be doing me a favour.

Chris   Still have to get it cleaned, though. There's no cleaning staff in until tomorrow –

Harry   I won't make a mess, I promise.

Chris   Well, there's a couple not getting here till nine or so –

Harry   That's marvellous.

Chris   Alright then.

Harry   Nice doing business with you.

Chris   You want to go up now?

Harry   Yeah, I smell of defeat. Not mine – other chap.

Harry *and* **Chris** *go to the door, just as* **Alistair** *comes in, roaring like a Sergeant Major.*

Alistair   Right then, you cock-sucking arsemonkeys, who's going to get on their knees and give me some fucking. . . . . head –

Alistair *simultaneously clocks that the room is half-empty, and that* **Chris** *is there. He holds out his hand to* **Chris***, switching instantly into charming.*

Hi. Alistair Ryle.

Chris   Hello.

Alistair   How d'you do.

Chris   Very well, thank you.

Alistair   Lovely pub. Alright, chaps?

Harry   Ryle.

Ed   Hi Alistair.

Alistair (*to* **Chris**)   Sorry about the, uh –

Chris   No no, heard it all before. Should hear Chef when he's cut his finger.

Harry   Chefs.

Alistair   This part of the original, in here?

Chris   Part of the original, yes.

Alistair   Very sympathetic.

Alistair *looks at* **Harry**.

Tab shoo?

Harry   Tab shoo. Going to get changed.

Alistair   Excellent, you stink. (*To* **Chris**.) Good to meet you.

Chris *and* **Harry** *go out.* **Alistair** *comes into the room, looking around. He sees* **Toby**'s *wig and points at it.*

Ah, the wig of shame.

Fuck this is a long way from town.

Ed   Banned from anywhere closer, aren't we, the radius. . .

Alistair   Taxi driver couldn't find it. Should've hired a minibus, all come together.

Ed   Yeah, all rock up together like Reservoir Dogs.

Alistair   Excited, Grasshopper?

Ed   Yeah.

Alistair   You should be.

The Riot Club rides again.

Alistair *lights a cigarette.*

Toby   Mate I don't know if we can –

Alistair   Private Dining room, that's the point, isn't it? Home from home.

Ed *takes out a packet of cigarettes and lights one.* **Toby** *opens a window. Voices are heard coming down the corridor.*

Listen.

Hugo (*off*)   Just give it one night, OK? Please.

Hugo *comes into the room, followed by* **Miles**.

Miles   It's not the –

Miles *sees the other boys in the room.*

Forget it, doesn't matter.

Hugo   Evening.

Toby   Oh look, it's the Magdalen Marys.

Ed   Hi Hugo. Miles.

Hugo *takes off his gloves.*

Hugo   Alliteration, Maitland? Last refuge of the scoundrel.

Toby   Pompous prick.

Hugo   And again? B-minus.

Where's James?

Alistair   Gaffer's not here yet.

Hugo   Huh. Unpresidented.

Alistair   So two new boys. How you feeling?

Ed   Awesome. Totes excited.

Alistair (*to* **Toby**)   He says totes.

Toby   Don't say totes, fucking parody of yourself.

Alistair   How'd you like your room makeover, Miles?

Hugo   Al, I wouldn't –

Miles   Well, it was *thorough*.

Ed   It was amazing, fucking savage –

Toby   Mate – doghouse, yeah?

Hugo   Doghouse is already occupied, Toby.

Toby   Only till the dregsing, mate.

Alistair   Sorry, Milo?

Miles   Didn't quite get the tails-hung-up thing, the symbolism.

Ed   What thing?

Miles   Where they hang your tails up on a hanger in the middle of the room. So when you walk in for a second it looks like someone hanged themself.

Ed   No way.

Alistair   Just a calling card.

Ed   Didn't do that in mine.

Toby   You haven't got a central light fitting.

Alistair   Why'd you get such a tiny room, anyway? Thought you'd get the set your brother had with the windows onto the quad.

Hugo   'The Montgomery Suite'.

Alistair   Awesome quad parties.

Ed   Ground floor, mate. Access requirements.

Hugo   Ah. The Monty Suite's been given to a disabled.

Alistair   Jesus fuck.

Ed   Well I wish you'd left me a calling card.

Miles   *I* wish they hadn't jizzed all over my fucking stuff.

The others turn to **Miles**.

Hugo   Milo –

Alistair   Mate?

Miles   Nothing.

Alistair   Is there a problem?

Miles   Well yeah, I –

Hugo   It's fine, he's just –

Miles   I didn't expect someone's semen all over my books.

Ed   Mate, it's part of the room trash – that's what happens.

Miles   It's actually really difficult to get off. Paper's porous.

Alistair   Didn't Hugo tell you? This is a club for getting fucked and fucking stuff up, mate.

Hugo   It's a bit more than that, I think you'll –

Ed   Don't they trash rooms at Harrow?

Miles   More of a sports club thing.

Alistair   No wait, don't tell me – your mates were all in bands . . .

Miles   Yeah.

Alistair   . . . and when you got to Oxford there was this one night in Freshers Week where you were sat in the college bar looking around at all your new friends who grew up in – help me, Tubes –

Toby   Stockport.

Alistair   Who grew up in Stockport or wherever, when this chap comes and sits next to you –

Toby   In a smoking jacket . . .

Hugo   Guys, don't –

Alistair   In a smoking jacket and he says something in Latin – which somehow cuts right to the heart of you . . .

Toby   Cause he seems to understand exactly – *exactly* – how you're feeling.

Alistair   And then he tells you the story of Lord Riot the famous Libertine. And he feeds you a drink of his favourite vintage Port – private supply – and he tells you he's in Lord Riot's club and you should come along.

Toby   It's very exclusive. Top secret.

Alistair   *Assentio mentium*: the meeting of minds.

Toby   And you're exactly the right sort of chap.

Alistair   Hugo Fraser-Tyrwhitt: Operation Pretty Boy.

Hugo   One word for you, Toby: *YouTube*.

Ed   Two words. No, sorry –

Toby   Oh my god, that one last year.

Alistair   Gay Harry Potter?

Toby   Couldn't afford his tails in the end so Hugo had to drop him.

Hugo   That's not what happened at –

Alistair   Gay Harry Potter.

Miles   I'm not gay, by the way.

Ed   It's OK to be gay.

Miles   I know, but I'm not, so – I think there's something fairly gay about wanking in someone's bedroom.

I'd also quite like to know whose jizz it is.

Alistair   Hugo?

Hugo   Well, it's. It's one for all and all for one.

Miles   Meaning what?

Hugo   Everyone takes part in the trashing, so in a way it's everyone's jizz.

Miles   You *all* wanked on my books?

Harry *comes in, looking immaculate in his tails.*

Alistair   Next year *you* get to do it to someone else.

Miles   I don't want to.

Harry   What are we talking about?

Toby   You do what the president tells you to do.

Hugo   You don't *have* to.

Toby   He's supposed to lead by example.

Miles   So James jizzed on my books?

Harry   Oh no, that was me. Always happy to whack one out for the good of the club.

Alistair *starts to pace the room, looking in the drawers of the sideboard.*

Toby   How was the room?

Harry   Three star.

Ed   D'you mess it up?

Harry   Did a big dump in the loo, got my money's worth. Release the otters!

Miles   Nice.

Toby   Come on Leighton, let's do this.

Hugo   Has he texted anyone?

They all whip out their phones and check.

Toby   Nope.

Hugo   No.

Harry (*reading a text*)   Excellent.

Toby   Mate?

Harry   No, something else, sorry.

Al, did Leighton text you?

Harry *looks at* **Alistair**, *sees he's reading from a burgundy leather-look binder which he found in one of the drawers.*

Ooh, what you got?

Alistair   'Your Private Dining Experience at the Bull's Head Inn, Kidsbury'

Harry   Gosh, are we having an experience?

Alistair   'Guests are invited to choose from three elegant three-course menus'.

Harry *charges towards* **Alistair**.

Harry   Let's have a look.

Alistair *holds the folder away so that* **Harry** *can't see it.*

Alistair   So the game is – Which One Did Leighton Pick?

Hugo   What do we call it, 'Meal of Fortune'?

Miles   'Meal or no Meal'.

Hugo   Excellent.

Alistair   Here, you be trolley dolly.

Alistair *holds the folder towards* **Miles**.

Ed   I'll do it.

Hugo   Go on, Miles.

Miles *comes forward and takes the folder from* **Alistair**.

Alistair   Good man.

Miles   Um, OK, Menu A:

Alistair   Just a bit of fun till the boss-man gets here.

Miles   Pâté Maison with melba toast, followed by breast of chicken wrapped in bacon with dauphinoise potatoes and a tarragon jus then seasonal berry pavlova.

Harry   It's the 80s retro menu!

Alistair   We are *not* having chicken.

Harry   What's menu B?

Guy *comes in, singing LMFAO: 'Party Rock Anthem'*

Guy   Party Rock is in the house tonight / Everybody just have a good time / And we gone make you lose your mind –

Toby   Bellingfield!

Harry   Bell-end!

Guy   We just wanna see ya SHAKE THAT –

Guy *does a robotic dance, beeping the tune, but gets distracted after a few moves:*

Where the fuck is Leighton?

Ed   Not here yet.

Guy   Sorry I'm late, chaps. Stuff to do.

Harry   Didn't miss you.

Guy   Harsh.

What we doing?

Hugo   Which menu did Leighton pick.

Alistair   Lovely assistant Milo – Menu B?

Miles   Um, tomato gazpacho,

Ed   Cold soup. So wrong.

Harry   Wait wait – Al, isn't gazpacho that red stuff you dip nachos in?

Alistair   No, mate, you're thinking of salsa.

Harry   Salsa? Why, isn't that a sort of dance?

Alistair   I don't know, you'll have to ask Bellingfield.

Guy   Fuck right off.

Toby   What's this?

Harry   Lauren's got Guy going to Salsa class.

Toby   Awesome.

Hugo   Very sensual.

Guy   All in the hips, mate, all about the hips.

Anyway, you don't need to –

Toby   Menu B! Come on!

Miles   Yeah, so gazpacho, then Assiette of Denby Farm pork. Three ways.

Harry   'Three way pork'? That is *filthy*.

Alistair   What's pudding?

Alistair *picks up* **Harry***'s fencing foil and starts to mime fighting with it.*

Miles   Chocolate Fondant.

Alistair   Risky. Like it.

Hugo   Menu C?

Miles   Um, carpaccio of beef with parmesan shavings and a rocket salad.

Toby   What's carpaccio mean?

Hugo   Raw beef, very thinly sliced.

Harry   That's so gay.

Miles   Then main course is Pan-fried Sea Bream with fennel salad and new potatoes.

Harry   Gay!

Alistair   Pudding?

Miles   Mango crème brulee.

Hugo   Burnt cream.

Harry   So gay. Menu C is the gay menu.

Alistair   So, fingers on buzzers, which one do we think Leighton picked?

Miles   Could have done a mash-up.

Guy   Leighton hasn't picked, though, so the game doesn't really –

Alistair   What?

Guy *comes to* **Miles** *and takes the menu out of his hands.*

Guy   Well, um – fact is, Leighton's delegated the menu this time.

Hugo   Delegated?

Guy   You know, he's got a lot on. OUCA, rowing practice, applying for int –

Al/Harry   Internships.

Harry   He's the Interninator.

Guy   Chap needed a hand so he uh, he asked me to take care of it.

Alistair   You?

Guy   Yeah.

Hugo   So which one did you pick?

Guy   I didn't –

Harry   You didn't pick and Leighton didn't pick – what?

Guy   No, it's. Special night, isn't it? Calls for a bespoke approach.

Hugo   It's not one of these menus?

Guy   It's *based* on one of those menus.

Harry   Which one?

Guy   Well it doesn't matter, cause it –

Alistair   Does matter – which one?

Guy   OK, menu A.

The others groan.

Guy   Chaps chaps chaps I've *customised* it, so –

Hugo   How?

Guy   Everything's gone a bit more Riot Club.

Hugo   How d'you make chicken a bit more Riot Club?

Guy   Well I don't want to tell you because – just trust me, it's going to be awesome.

Hugo   How d'you *customise* a pavlova?

Miles   Sparklers?

Guy   OK, look, if I tell you about pudding can we put the menus away?

Alistair   Course, yeah.

Guy   So, OK, so it says seasonal berry pavlova on the menu – but we're not from the 80s, yeah, we're from the *now*, so – so I look at that and think OK, work with it, make it celebrate our awesomeness, our back-in-business-ness – ness.

Toby   So?

Guy   So how d'you make an Eton Mess?

Harry   Tell him he only got into Bristol?

Guy   OK, Eton Mess is basically you get a pavlova and then you smash it up with a hammer, right? Far as I'm concerned that's the Riot Club in a pudding.

The boys think.

Just wait till you see the main course.

Chris *opens the door to usher someone in.*

Chris   Just through here.

Dimitri *strides into the room, wearing Riot Club tails, plus a scarf and a vintage-style leather helmet and goggles. It's not immediately obvious to the others who he is. He looks like a cross between* **Mr Toad** *and Biggles.*

Toby   What the f –

Dimitri *puts his goggles on top of his head with a flourish, then stands with his hands on his hips.*

Dimitri   Evening chaps.

The boys laugh, recognising him. **Guy** *goes over to shake his hand / man-hug him.*

Guy   Dims, mate.

Hugo   Dimitri, you absolute –

Dimitri   Good to be back, boys. Good to be back.

Guy *puts the menu folder back in a drawer.*

Chris   Um lads, is that smoke I can smell?

Alistair   Smoke? I don't think so. Can anybody smell smoke?

Harry   Maybe someone outside, I don't know.

Chris   If you want to smoke there's a patio at the back.

Toby   Can't we just blow it out the window?

Harry   Tubes.

Chris   No sign of Mr Leighton yet?

Dimitri   James isn't here?

Harry   He hasn't called you?

Chris   Nope, nothing. Hoping we'd get started on time, I've got another big party in the restaurant, Ruby Wedding.

Guy   Can I have a word, actually?

Chris   Um, yes.

Guy   Guy Bellingfield – we spoke on the phone about the food.

Chris   Yes, of course.

Guy   Just wanted a quick word about how you're going to serve it.

Chris   Yes, I thought we'd bring it in on a –

Guy   Out of earshot? – so sorry, don't want to spoil the surprise.

Chris   Right, course.

Chris *and* **Guy** *leave the room.*

Alistair   Seriously, why would James delegate the food to Bell-end? All he ate at school was potatoes.

Harry'*s phone rings.*

Dimitri   With ketchup.

Harry *answers the phone.*

Harry   Hello? Hi, yeah.

Alistair   The man has no palate.

Harry   No, we're here. No, not the Bull. The Bull's Head. Kidsbury, yeah.

Harry *leaves the room, putting a cigarette in his mouth as he goes.*

Ed   Thought we weren't supposed to take phone calls.

Toby   More importantly – Dimitri?

Dimitri   Yeah?

Toby   The fuck have you got on your head?

Dimitri   Just came here on the bike.

Alistair   What bike?

Dimitri   1962 Triumph Thunderbird.

Miles   You've got a Thunderbird?

Dimitri   Bought it yesterday.

Ed   Is it like in The Great Escape?

Dimitri *takes off his goggles and helmet and puts them on the table.*

Dimitri   No, because that's American. This is a classic British bike. 650cc.

Hugo   How long till you drive it into a pond?

Dimitri   I'm a good driver.

Hugo   Not going to be a good driver by the end of dinner – how you going to ride it home?

Dimitri   Whack it in the back of the minibus.

Guy *comes back into the room, tuning back into the conversation.*

Toby   Yeah, but sometimes they send a people carrier, Space Cruiser thing – can't fit a motorbike –

Dimitri   They're not going to send a Space Cruiser.

Toby   How d'you know?

Dimitri   Cause I booked it myself. It's definitely a minibus.

Guy   You booked it?

Dimitri   Nothing but the best for my boys.

Guy   How come you booked it?

Dimitri   You're looking at tonight's official Post-Party Party Starter. Seeing as how we're back with a capital *boom*, James has put me in charge of organising something suitably awesome.

Hope you've got your shades, chaps, you're gonna be up till dawn.

Hugo   What, tequila shots on Port Meadow?

Dimitri   Now did I say we were staying in Oxford?

Guy   Oh my god.

Dimitri   Got to keep Tubes out of town, haven't we? Away from girls with camera phones.

Toby   Yeah yeah.

Alistair   So where we going?

Dimitri   Surprise!

Now, who wants a sit on the motorbike?

Ed   Me! Me!

Hugo   I'll give it a miss, if you don't mind.

Dimitri *holds up his keys.*

Dimitri   Your loss. Anyone got a licence?

Miles   Yeah, I have.

Hugo   Have you?

Miles   Yeah.

Dimitri   Go for your life.

Dimitri *hands the keys to* **Miles***.* **Miles** *heads out of the door, followed by* **Toby***,* **Ed***,* **Alistair**. . . *and* **Hugo***.*

Toby   Thought you were sitting out.

Hugo   Have a smoke while I'm out there, can't I?

Guy   James gave you the job?

Dimitri   Well, you know. Volunteered.

Guy   After I told you I was going to talk to him?

Dimitri   Like you said, elections next term, no harm in helping out a bit, upping one's profile . . .

Guy   I said that about me, I didn't think you'd be –

Dimitri   All those ideas you got from your uncle.

Guy   Yeah, ideas *I* got.

Dimitri *shrugs.*

So what, you're getting us all on a flight to Vienna?

Dimitri   Wait and see.

Guy   Fuck I wish I hadn't told you.

Dimitri   Why did you? If you didn't want me to have a go as well?

Guy   Because you're my friend.

Dimitri   Tactical error, mate.

Guy   Yeah, but I didn't think you'd –

Dimitri   What?

Guy   I didn't think you'd be going for president.

Dimitri   You think I wouldn't be a good president?

Guy   No, I just –

Dimitri   Is it cos I is Greek?

Guy   No, god. No.

Dimitri   Jesus, Bellingfield. It's because I'm Greek?

Guy   No, I mean – No, in a lot of ways you're more English than any of us –

Dimitri   What, it's in the statutes I have to produce four British grandparents, or –

Guy   No.

Dimitri   You think I can't be President because I'm Greek!

Guy   Mate, mate, really I – I'm not being –

Dimitri   Game on, mate. Game on.

Dimitri *takes a stack of bank notes out of his pocket, and during the following places one bank note under each of the place mats on the table.*

Guy   What – what you doing?

Dimitri   All part of the surprise.

Guy   Fuck's sake –

Alistair *and* **Harry** *come back in, in high spirits.*

Alistair   Mate, that is fucking *magnificent.*

Harry   Those guys knew how to live, you know? Want it, woof it.

Harry *clocks the atmosphere in the room.*

Fuck, it's every time I walk in.

Alistair (*to* **Harry**)   Mate, tell the guys what you just told me.

Dimitri   Bell-end wants to be president.

Alistair   What?

Harry   We've got a president.

Dimitri   Bell-end's *campaigning* for next time.

Guy   So are you!

Alistair   Can you stop hacking for two seconds?

Villiers.

Harry   So yeah, I'm talking to this chap I met at Cowes, turns out he's a Riot Club member from back in the roaring 80s. And apparently – at one of the most legendary dinners ever – apparently they hired a girl.

Guy   A girl?

Harry   Prozzer. Kept her under the table – sucked cocks all night.

Alistair   Fucking hell.

Harry   Went round under the table, one at a time. Possibly more than one at a time, I mean she's got two hands – you know . . .

Guy   Oh my god.

Dimitri   Chlamydia anyone?

Harry It's fine, mate, I've booked a clean one, she'll bring paperwork. It's a reputable agency.

Guy   Wait – what – hang on –

Dimitri You've *actually* booked one?

Harry She'll be here before pudding.

Alistair, **Guy** *and* **Dimitri** *crease up laughing.*

Alistair   Isn't that fucking awesome?

Dimitri   Wait, is this you bidding for President?

Harry   President? Fuck no.

I'm just bringing sexy back.

Guy *and* **Dimitri** *glare at each other.*

Alistair   Does James know?

Harry   Not the specifics.

Toby *and* **Ed** *barrel back into the room, followed by* **Hugo** *and* **Miles** *– they're all on a motorbike-induced high.*

Toby   That is a savage bike, mate.

Ed   Savage.

Dimitri   What d'you think, Huge?

Hugo   Quite stylish, isn't it, as big lumps of metal go.

Miles   So Ed's got an idea where we might be going in the minibus.

Ed   Are we going to London? Rock up at Mahiki or –

Dimitri   No, we're not going to London.

Ed   Edinburgh?

Dimitri   You've all got your passports back at college, yeah?

Miles   God, are we really going somewhere?

Toby   We're going *abroad*?

Dimitri   Club tradition, apparently. The after-dinner *jaunt*. Don't know why we got out of the habit.

Alistair   So where we going?

Guy   Vienna.

Dimitri   We can do better than Vienna.

Guy   Marrakech.

Dimitri   Nice idea – next time.

Guy   Burma, Cambodia, the Lebanon.

Toby   Fuck yeah, let's go to the Lebanon!

Harry   And the mission is to boff someone in a Burqa.

Hugo   That's going to take a while, isn't it – get there, presumably buy a ticket –

Dimitri   We're not going to an airport.

Harry   Oh mate. Mummy's little runaround?

Dimitri   Yup.

Miles   What?

Harry   The Mitropoulos family jet.

Ed   A private jet to the Lebanon!

Miles   Fuck.

Dimitri   We're not going to the Lebanon, OK? We're going somewhere else.

James *hurries in, carrying a rucksack. His shirt is untucked at the front and his bow tie is crooked.*

James   Sorry, evening chaps, so sorry.

Dimitri   James, where've you –

Ed   Hi James.

James   Numerical reasoning test.

Alistair   On a Saturday?

James   Had to wait for all the others to finish counting on their fingers.

Alistair   Standard.

James   Landlord was being a bit funny – no one's told him we're the Riot Club, have they?

Hugo   He was being funny cause you look like you just crawled out of an Oxfam clothes bin.

Hugo *comes over to* **James** *and straightens his bow tie for him while* **James** *tucks in his shirt.*

James   Had to change in the taxi, couldn't do the test in my tails, could I? 'Sorry, got to leave early, going to a Riot Cl . . .

James *sees* **Chris** *come in over* **Hugo***'s shoulder.*

. . . Young Entrepreneurs dinner'

Hi there.

Chris   Hi – d'you mind if we get started pretty quick –

James   Not at all. So sorry –

Chris   Don't want the timing to be off for your main course.

James   No, absolutely.

Chris   Just redoing the toast for your starters. You're all here now, yes?

James   Yes, aren't we?

James *does a quick head count.*

Eight.

Dimitri   And you.

James   Nine. Who's missing?

Guy   Balf's still in the bar – I'll get him.

Guy *goes out to the bar. The boys start to arrange themselves around the table.*

Chris   And could I possibly take a card to swipe through the machine?

James   Yeah, absolutely.

James *pulls a card out of out his wallet.*

Hugo   James – which end?

James *points to the end of the table he intends to sit at, then hands a card to* **Chris***.*

James   Here you go, put it on that one. Social fund.

Hugo (*pointing to the seat next to him*)   Milo – you're here.

Chris *inserts* **James***' card into a hand-held payment machine and stands near the door waiting for it to work.*

Future captains of industry, then, are you?

James   Some of us, yeah.

Chris   Alan Sugars of tomorrow.

George *and* **Guy** *come back in.*

George   Here I am chaps, never fear! (*To* **James***.*) Where d'you want me?

James   Up here.

Chris (*to* **James***)   Just need your PIN number . . .

Chris *hands the machine to* **James** *who types in his PIN.*

George   Um, it's actually just 'PIN'.

Chris   Sorry?

George   The N stands for number, it's Personal Identification Number, so if you say PIN Number, you're actually saying Number twice.

James   George –

George   You're saying Personal Identification Number Number.

Dimitri   Mate, come on.

James   Have you had a drink?

Chris   I'm sorry, I didn't –

George (*to* **James**)   Couple of pints, yeah, but I wasn't in the room yet.

(*To* **Chris**.) Sorry, totally didn't mean that in a rude way, just my father always says it to me, so –

James *hands the machine back to* **Chris**.

James   I do apologise.

Toby (*to* **George**)   You're going to be wasted.

George   Chaps like that offer you a drink, you don't say no thanks.

Ed   You could say P.I. Number.

Harry   Move on, mate.

Toby   Dims, can Ed sit with you? Please?

Alistair   Get on well with the Wurzels, did you?

George   Turns out one of them used to work for my father, then he got his own farm, free-range piggies, did terribly well till the economy went, well, tits. Bloody nice chap, too. Shame.

George *finds his place among the boys – they're all standing around the table now, with one space free at the head of the table for* **James**. *A slight hush descends.*

Chris *tears off* **James**' *receipt and hands his card back to him.*

Chris   There you go, all done.

James   Thanks very much. OK.

James *comes to the table.* **Chris** *sees the boys' silence and interprets it as his cue.*

Chris   Right then. Well, evening gentlemen – welcome to the
Bull's Head, very glad to have you here this evening, hope you'll
have a great night.

Please sit down – make yourselves at home . . .

The boys all look at **James** *– they can't sit before the president. He
considers for a moment, but it's too complicated to explain the
protocol to* **Chris***, so he sits.*

The others are hesitant, looking at **James***.*

James (*almost under his breath*)   Sit down, guys.

The others sit.

Chris   Great. So just a bit of housekeeping before we start
serving your dinner. Firstly, this might be a private dining room,
but I'm afraid you can't smoke in here. If you do want to pop out
there's a patio out the back – you just go out of here, down the
corridor to the left and through the fire door. Which is also your
fire exit. And there's a lavatory just adjacent, for your private use
so you don't have to go through the main bar to access the
facilities.

Now, hope you're all hungry, no vegetarians around the table, I
trust.

Toby   Villiers only eats pussy.

James   No, there's no vegetarians.

Chris   And you want to go straight onto the wine, and leave the
champagne until later, yes?

Hugo   We've got plans for the champagne.

Chris   Let's get some wine going, then –

Chris *goes to the sideboard and picks up a bottle of wine already
open there.*

Hugo (*to* **Guy**)   Wait, you've chosen the wine already?

Chris (*to* **Guy**)   Would you care to taste it?

Hugo   Who made you Bottlemeister?

Guy   Goes with the job of the food. Problem?

Hugo   Like asking a builder to do a Faberge egg.

Guy   D'you want to try it?

A murmur of anticipation goes around the table.

George   Careful, Huge.

Hugo *looks at the others, narrowing his eyes. They look back challengingly.*

Hugo   I'll happily. Test it.

The boys silently watch as **Chris** *goes to* **Hugo** *and pours a little wine into his glass.*

Chris   Bought this in specially, we don't normally have it.

Guy   Bespoke service.

There is almost an intake of breath as **Hugo** *slowly lifts the glass to his mouth. But instead of drinking it, he breathes deeply, inhaling the smell.*

The boys breathe out, suppressing giggles.

Hugo *looks at the label on the bottle in* **Chris'** *hand.*

Hugo   Bordeaux? Odd choice.

Guy   Bourgogne. Burgundy.

Hugo   It isn't.

Chris *looks at the label on the wine.*

Chris   Oh heck, sorry, bottles must have got mixed up.

James   What's the problem?

Guy   No no, don't worry – can we just pour the right one instead?

Toby   What's wrong with that wine?

Chris   Yeah, it's still in the cellar, though.

Dimitri   It's the wrong one.

Toby   It's wine, isn't it?

Dimitri   There's a different wine for each course, yeah?

Guy   D'you think we could fetch it, the right one?

Dimitri   So what's happened is Bellingfield's gone the extra mile and got a pre- dinner wine as well. Because he's *awesome*.

James   What's wrong with the wine, Huge?

Hugo   Just a bit Christmassy for this stage of the meal.

Guy   It's not *for* this stage of the meal, it's for the main course, it'll go perfectly –

The boys look to **James***, in need of a decision.*

Hugo   We should be drinking the right one, shouldn't we, Leighton?

Chris   How about I just swap them – serve this now and the other one later?

George   They're both made out of grapes, right?

Guy   No, but Leighton –

James   Pour it, thank you.

Chris   Righto. Sorry about that.

Chris *starts to go around the table, pouring the wine.*

James   Don't worry, happens to the best of us.

Dimitri   Oh dear, Bellingfield. Awkward.

Chris *is close to* **Alistair** *and jostles his elbow slightly as he leans in to pour his wine.*

Chris   Oh, sorry.

Alistair *takes the bottle from* **Chris***.*

Alistair   Please – may I?

Chris   Want to be a waitress, do you?

Alistair   Sommelier.

Chris   OK, well.

James *stands up, ushers* **Chris** *towards the door.*

James   Thanks Chris, that's great.

Chris   Your starters'll be along in a minute. Just ask if there's anything else you need.

James   Thank you. Thanks everso much.

Chris *leaves.* **James** *shuts the door behind him, then turns around to the others:*

Gentlemen – let's do this.

George   Hurrah!

Toby   Fuck yeah!

They all jump up and stand behind their chairs again. **James** *walks back to the head of the table.*

The bottle of wine is passed around and empty glasses filled.

Guy   Can I just say that was his fuckup about the wine, not mine?

Dimitri   Mate, it just got a bit complicated.

Hugo   Smells like good wine, it'll be great with the Chicken Kiev –

Guy   It's not –

Hugo   Or whatever the big surprise is.

James   OK, starting blocks, chaps, know you're all raring to go. Nice work, Hugo, dodging a scrunch for drinking before the president.

Hugo   I thank you.

Toby   Come on, let's go!

James   Let's have a bit of order, yeah? Remember this isn't a democracy.

The boys laugh and quieten down.

So. Good evening gentlemen, welcome to the Bull's Head. My name's James Leighton-Masters and I'll be your president for this evening. Now, just a bit of *housekeeping* to go through with you. . . .

Various shouts of 'Boo!' **James** *pulls out a roll of black bin liners, and holds it up, then throws it to the other end of the table.*

. . . before we start on the proper business of the evening: getting chateaued beyond belief.

The others applaud and whoop, banging the table in delight.
James *tears one bag off the roll and hands it round the table – they each take a bag and pass it on to the next boy.*

Now, don't forget there's no leaving the room till after dinner – if you do need a piss at any point, you'll notice there's plenty of pot plants. Or you can do it out the window if it's more than a quick wazz.

We've been a while in the wilderness, gentlemen, thanks to our bewigged friend over here – who we'll be dealing with later –

Hugo   Not having a dregsing, are we?

Toby   Bring it on. Two pints of milk.

George   God I've missed this.

James   Two terms without a dinner, boys, two whole terms out in the cold. Let's just say it hasn't been easy. But we've weathered the storm, kept our heads down, our beaks clean and our faces out of the papers and we have been handsomely rewarded. Summoned back to the table, to do what we do best.

Ed   Yay!

James   Oh, on the proviso that we keep it quiet this time.

Alistair   Boo!

James   'Keep it contained' – I was told – 'I'll do what I can', I said, 'but hey, all the boys want is to have the evening they *deserve* – and if they want to raise the roof, how could I possibly stop them?'

The others laugh.

'How can one man stand against the might of the fucking Riot Club?'

The others bang the table in agreement.

There's a new wind blowing, gentlemen. The time for mourning is past, no more beating our breasts and howling at the moon. Now is the time to throw off our chains, to dance footloose upon the earth, to carpe some fucking diem. We've earned tonight, gentlemen. We've earned it.

So, in the name of all that is riotous, let us eat till we explode,

George   Huzzah!

James   Drink till our eyes fall out,

Toby   Hear hear!

Harry   Yes!

James   And leave a trail of glorious destruction in our wake.

The boys clap and cheer.

Hugo, will you kindly lead the President's Toast?

Hugo *stands up and raises his glass to* **James**.

Hugo   We who are about to dine, salute you.

All   Cenaturi Te Salutant.

James   Gentlemen – imbibe.

The boys all drink to **James***, draining their glasses then slamming them down. There's a moment while they take a breath – some of them reel from the alcohol, some reach for the bottles and fill the glasses up again. The party has started.*

Dimitri (*to* **James**)   Mate, are we singing?

James   Yeah yeah, we're doing it now.

Guy   So patriotic, it's sweet.

James   Hugo?

The boys prepare to sing. **Hugo** *gives the first note.*

Hugo   Maaaaaaaah.

The boys pick up the note and sing the national anthem.

Chris *opens the door to bring in the starters, but hesitates because of the singing. He nods in approval, then joins in. The boys turn to look, and with the shock their singing peters out.* **Chris** *is left singing God Save The Queen on his own, with a plate of pâté de foie gras in each hand.*

Blackout.

Scene Three

Later. The boys are finishing their pâté. **George** *is standing up.*

Dimitri   Don't know, just a slightly odd texture.

Guy   If you don't like it, don't eat it.

Dimitri   Just a bit gritty, that's all.

James   I don't think it's gritty.

Guy   Ironic really. Cousins in Greece eating *actual grit* right now.

Ed   Have they run out of houmous?

Toby   Debt crisis, you wad.

George   I'll eat it. Woofed mine down already. Yum, Bellingfield.

Dimitri *and* **George** *swap plates.*

Dimitri   Just had better, that's all.

Guy   What, wrapped in a vine leaf?

Hugo (*to* **Guy**)   Will you be enlightening us as to the metaphorical import? Or is it just 'the Riot Club in a pâté'?

Dimitri What's this?

Hugo Guy's menu. Everything's got a special symbolic significance.

Dimitri Oh, this is classic.

Guy Foie gras: it's hedonism, isn't it – the ultimate extravagance. That's what we stand for.

Dimitri Classic.

Ed I thought that was caviar.

Dimitri Don't they force-feed them?

Guy What?

Dimitri The geese, yeah? Force-feed them till they get massively distended livers?

Hugo Gavage.

Dimitri Awesome metaphor, mate.

George Uh, chaps, still waiting here.

James Guys, yeah, sorry – everyone finished? Balf's doing the Lady Anne.

The boys quieten down and listen. **Miles** *goes to stand up, but* **Hugo** *stops him.*

Hugo We sit for this one.

George Gentlemen:

George *raises his glass.*

the Lady Anne.

Hugo Is that it?

George What?

Hugo You're not going to say anything about her beauty or –

George Not so good with the wordy stuff, I –

Ed   Who's Lady Anne?

Hugo   Lord Riot's girlfriend, mistress whatever, the one he was in love with.

James   Don't worry about it Balf, it's fine.

Hugo   No, it's – if it weren't for Lady Anne, the club wouldn't exist, would it?

Dimitri *goes to stand up.*

Dimitri   I'll do it.

James   Not this one, Dims.

Dimitri   What, too dusky for you?

Miles   Why can't Dimitri do it?

Alistair   Have to be titled.

Guy   God, protocol, Dims.

Ed   I thought *Lord Riot* started the club.

George   Guys I would dearly love to eat this pate.

Hugo   Do the toast properly, then. Extemporise.

Ed   So the club was started by a *girl*?

Hugo   Riot's *friends* started the club to honour his memory.

James   Sit down, Balf.

Hugo   No. It's supposed to be a moving tribute to her finer qualities, yes?

George   OK, um. Well. She was very very beautiful and very very nice and I think any of us would have been lucky to have the opportunity to fight a duel for her, um, honour, though I think I probably wouldn't have got a second glance off her, being as I am, a bit of a tool.

Harry   Oh, mate.

George   The Lady Anne.

All   The Lady Anne.

They all drink the wine down in one and slam the empty glass down on the table. They reach for the bottles and fill the glasses up again.

Ed   So Lord Riot was never *in* the Riot Club?

Toby   Fuck's sake what's wrong with you –

Miles   When did the smashing start?

Chris *and* **Rachel** *come in.*

Chris   We clear these plates out of your way, lads?

James   Absolutely.

Several of the boys stand up as **Rachel** *comes into the room.*

Chris   This is Rachel – she'll be helping me out serving you this evening.

Harry   Hello.

James   Hello Rachel.

Rachel   Please, you don't need to –

Ed   Hi Rachel.

Guy   Sorry, Dimitri would like to know if you've got any Taramasalata hanging about.

George   Yeah, chap needs his fish eggs, d'you have any?

James   Guys –

Chris   Um, Rachel, have we got any taramasalata?

Rachel   No Dad.

George   Or any Euros?

Ed   Dad! Is he your dad?

Chris   Rachel's my daughter, yes.

Guy   We need pitta bread and Euros!

Rachel   It's a joke, Dad – I think he's Greek.

Toby   Yeah, jokes.

Dimitri   Sorry, Rachel – trouble with Guy is he's *hilarious*.

James   Did we mention the pâté was excellent?

Hugo   Exemplary!

Chris   Thanks very much. Michael will be chuffed. The chef.

Harry   So, father and daughter team, then?

Rachel   Yeah, Frank and Nancy Sinatra.

Ed   Like Miley Cyrus and. Miley Cyrus's dad.

Chris   Just passing through, aren't you love? – she's got a degree.

Rachel   Oh, everyone's got a degree, Dad –

Chris   Job market, you know?

James   Yeah, tough, isn't it?

Chris   I mean you'd think she'd just walk into something, with a first.

Rachel (*to* **Toby**)   You finished?

Toby *blinks, flustered.*

Toby   Wuuurm – I mean yeah.

Hugo   A first? Felicitations.

George   Which college, Rachel?

Rachel   Newcastle.

George   Is that near LMH?

Harry   Mate, some people go to universities that aren't Oxford.

George   Oh yeah.

Harry   Sorry, he's had a very sheltered life.

Chris   She could have gone to Oxford, didn't want to.

James   Full of idiots like this lot, isn't it?

Harry   What d'you read?

Rachel   Modern Languages.

Harry   You'd need to up there, wouldn't you?

Rachel   Yeah, French, Spanish and Geordie.

Ed   Geordie Studies!

Guy (*crap Geordie accent*)   Weer's me Newky Brown?

Miles   I'm sorry about this.

George   That was really excellent pâté – I had two, so –

Chris   Thank you.

Guy   Rachel, did you drink Newky Brown?

Rachel   Only for breakfast.

Rachel *leans in to pick up* **Harry***'s plate.*

Harry   Chanel. Coco Mademoiselle.

Rachel   Yes. Well done.

Chris *and* **Rachel** *are finished collecting the plates.*

Chris   OK, your main course'll be along in a minute.

Dimitri   What's the main course?

Chris *goes to answer, and* **Guy** *has to cut him off.*

Chris   It's a –

Guy   SURPRISE! Still a surprise, remember.

Chris   Yes, of course, sorry.

James   Don't mind them – all a bit high-spirited.

Ed   'Bye Rachel.

Chris *and* **Rachel** *leave.* **Guy** *gets up to close the door behind them.*

Guy   Nice try, Dims.

Dimitri   I'm nearly coming in my pants from the expectation.

James *stands up.*

James   Right chaps – Banbury Toasts, while we're still upright.

Ed   That girl is tasty.

Guy   No chance mate, if Villiers saw her first.

The others all stand.

Ed   He's already had a blowjob today.

James *points at* **Harry**, *accusingly.*

James   Yeah, and scrunching Harry Villiers for sharking the waitress.

The boys jeer. **Harry** *holds up his glass.*

Toby   No sharking at the table.

Harry   The *delectable* waitress!

The boys laugh and chant 'scrunch scrunch scrunch' as **Harry** *drains his glass and then refills it.*

Ed   Legend.

James *raises his glass.*

James   OK, our next toast – which is to the many, many great men who have sat around this table before us. Gentlemen, raise your glasses to the dead members.

All   Dead members.

They down their drinks, then fill the glasses again.

Dimitri   You've got a dead member, haven't you, Leighton? Or is it just in a coma cause you haven't used it in so long?

James   Only cause your mum's been out of the country.

Guy   No shortage of penis-action once the prozzer gets here.

George   Anyone got some WD40 for Leighton?

James   Once the what gets here?

Harry   The prozzer.

James   You booked a prozzer?

Harry   Ho yus.

James   Fucking hell.

Hugo   What's he done?

Miles   I think he's hired a prostitute.

Harry   Thought we could stick her under the table, go round one at a time.

Alistair   What time's she booked?

Harry   Half past soon.

Ed   That is savage.

Hugo   Oh Villiers, that's so you.

Harry   She'll be under the table. I asked her to bring a false moustache for when she does you.

James   Mate, are you serious? This is –

Toby   This is fucking awesome!

George   Oh my wow.

James   We're supposed to be keeping it –

Harry   What?

James   Michael Bingham – I promised him we'd, you know, rein it in a bit.

Harry   There's precedent – acceptable in the 80s.

Ed   Who's Michael Bingham?

Guy   Ex-member. Keeps an eye on stuff.

Alistair   God, the fucking alumniati. You've had your moment, guys.

James   Yeah, but –

Guy   Don't be a pussy, Leighton.

Hugo   Sure it's not too late to cancel.

Harry   Reclaiming our heritage, isn't it?

Alistair   The evening we deserve, you said.

Dimitri   Yeah, back in business, carpe some fucking diem.

Alistair   Look, Bingham's never going to know, is he?

Harry   It's a discreet agency, I did check. Who's going to find out? Are we celebrating or are we celebrating?

Dimitri   *I'm* celebrating.

James   OK, OK.

Fuck it, what they don't know won't hurt them.

There's a general eruption of jollity.

Harry   Excellent.

George   Huge – Tyrwhitt – Hugo – (*To* **James**.) Is Hugo doing the Members Ex –

James   Yeah. Guys – guys – listen up –

Time for the most important toast of all, the Members Extant. Hugo

Fraser-Tyrwhitt.

Miles   We're toasting *ourselves*?

The others applaud. **Hugo** *bows, enjoying the attention.*

Hugo   Thank you, thank you. So to put this in context for our newest initiates, back in the very olden days the pause between courses were typically taken up with the recital of poetry, a habit we've rather fallen out of –

Ed Poetry?

Hugo Wrote it themselves, yes. Imagine a sonnet written by Villiers.

Harry 'Shall I compare thee to a bummer's arse?'

Hugo If Villiers had any wit.

On this of all nights, I see no reason why we shouldn't take a turn for the *iambic*, since we're dwelling on past as well as future glories. Permit me, then, to summon the spirit of another age, one of wine, women and so – *liloquy*.

Hugo *assumes a dramatic pose and begins to recite his poem.*

Once more unto the drink, dear friends, once more,
And give a roar for all our English drunk.
In peace there's nothing so becomes a man
As Milo's sweetness and sobriety;
But when the call to drink rings in his ears,
He'll imitate the action of the Tubester;
Stiffen the member, summon up the sword,
Disguise understanding with hard-drinking rage;
Then look like Guy with terrible aspect;
Burning eyes 'neath the wiggage of the head
Like the George Balfour; let the brow o'erwhelm it
As fearfully as does a Grecian frown
O'erhang and jutty poor Dimitri's face,
Steeped in the wild and wanton Ouzo.
Now be like Ryle and stretch the gullet wide,
Be Harry the brave, and hold up every sabre
To its full height. On, on you noblest Riot,
Whose blood is fet from vodka 80 proof!
Drinkers that, like so many Old Etonians
Have in these parts from morn till even drank,
Then drank some more for love of Leighton.
Dishonour not dead members; now attest
That Knights like our Lord Riot did beget you.
Be envy now to clubs of weaker blood,
And teach them how to drink. The game's afoot!

Pour out the spirits, and with glasses charged
Cry, 'God for Harry, Dimitri and Alistair, James, Toby, Edward,
Milo, Hugo, Guy and George!'

Hugo *ends on a roar and the others break into rapturous applause.*
Hugo *has a big drink, feeling great about himself. He sits down
and the others slap him on the back, joyfully.*

The door is flung open and **Chris** *comes in wheeling a trolley, on
top of which is a huge roast.*

Guy   Whoa – whoa – Gentlemen, pray silence for the main
course.

George   Oh my Christ. What is that?

Alistair   It's magnificent.

Chris   Bit of a monster, isn't it?

James   *What* is it?

Guy   What you're looking at, gentlemen, is a *ten bird roast*.

Chris   Actually, it's a –

Guy   Shake my hand.

Chris *shakes* **Guy***'s hand.*

Good man.

Chris   Thanks. Thank you.

Dimitri   It's not grotesque at all.

Ed   What's a ten bird roast?

Guy   Exactly what it says – a bird inside a bird inside a bird
inside a bird. Etc.

Harry   Roasted.

Hugo   It's what they ate at the first ever dinner.

Guy   Exactly – heritage.

Hugo (*to* **Miles**)   What d'you think?

Miles   Pretty impressive.

Guy   Cause there's ten of us, you see. It's one for all – i.e. one bird for each of us – and all for one – i.e. those ten birds bound together in the heat of the fire – the fire being our recent adversity – bound together in the heat of the adversity-fire into one entity. I.e. the club.

Dimitri   Impeccable logic there.

What birds is it?

Guy   Well, chicken for a start –

George   Must be something tiny in the middle or you've nowhere to go.

Ed   Quail maybe?

Harry   Poussin?

Chris   Woodcock, isn't it?

George   Woodcock are tiny. Bugger to shoot at.

Dimitri   Seriously, what birds is it?

Chris   Biggest turkey we could find, and the others are all inside.

Alistair   So what, you just stuff them inside each other?

Dimitri   Tell me what the other birds are.

Chris   Some of them get de-boned.

George   Yeah, they'd have to be.

Dimitri   I think we'd all like to know, Guy.

Guy   God, OK, it's um, (*he counts on his fingers*) Poussin,

Miles   No, woodcock.

Guy   Woodcock. Duck, chicken, goose, grouse, quail, partridge, turkey um um. *Pigeon*, pheasant, that's ten.

Chris   It's not a grouse, it's a guinea fowl.

George   Ah, guinea fowl, yes.

Chris   Except we didn't –

George   So they're de-boned and then wrapped around each other, are they?

Toby   Spatchcock!

George   What, mate?

Toby   No, just that, really.

Alistair   Bet the Stoics never had a ten bird roast.

Harry   It really is incredible. (*To* **Guy**.) Well done, mate.

Chris   Took two of us to get it sewn up and in the oven.

Hugo   Hats off, Guy, that's no Chicken Kiev.

Chris (*to* **Guy**)   Now I know you specified ten birds –

Toby   When we cut through it, will it be like rings of meat?

Guy   You'll see.

What d'you reckon, Balf?

George   It's amazing. Bellingfield – it's amazing.

Guy   Alright, is it, Leighton?

James   Bravo, mate. Good work.

Chris *looks around at the others.*

Chris   OK, who's going to carve?

Harry *stands up.*

Harry   How about I do it. . .

He takes the ornamental sabre and draws it with a flourish.

. . . with this?

The boys clap, cheer and bang the table.

Blackout.

Scene Four

Later. The boys are finishing their main courses, with the remains of the enormous roast on the table in front of them.

The atmosphere is considerably more subdued than before.

Toby *lifts his plate and smashes it down on the edge of the table.*

Toby   *Nine* fucking birds.

Guy   Yeah, OK, but. It's still nine birds.

Toby   How is a nine bird roast awesome?

George   I think it's delicious.

Miles   You're eating giblets.

George   Best bit. Delicious.

Alistair   Did he tell you it was only nine birds?

Guy   No, he didn't.

Alistair   Then we should complain.

Miles   Are we sure we counted right?

Hugo   Balf knows his game.

George   Definitely nine birds there.

Ed   Unless there was, like, a blue tit smashed up in the stuffing.

Alistair   If he made me eat a blue tit, I'll fucking sue.

James   Come on – it was totally cool.

Dimitri   Well, 90% cool.

Guy   What do they eat in the Lebanon? Squirrel kebab?

Dimitri   We're not going to the fucking –

James   What's this?

Dimitri   Nothing, it's –

James   We're going to the Lebanon?

Toby   Nine birds!

Dimitri   I mean, let me get this right, Bell-end – if the birds are *us*, actually we're saying one of us doesn't exist, so who's the invisible guinea fowl, who's that supposed to be?

Guy   OK, so maybe the *metaphor*'s gone a bit wobbly, but –

Dimitri   Mate, without the metaphor, it's just a pile of meat.

James   It's seriously not that big a thing.

Dimitri   It sort of is, though. Bellingfield planned this extremely carefully – ten birds, one for each of us – what that man's done is pissed all over Bell-end's beautiful plan.

He's basically made Guy's best idea *ever* into something pretty disappointing.

George   Hey, what's pudding going to be?

Miles   A ten-cake cake.

Alistair   It's not just the metaphor, it's the principle. We paid for a ten bird roast, we didn't get a ten bird roast.

George   Yeah, Bellingfield – what's for pudding? Is it a ten-cake cake?

James   It fed all of us.

Guy   No, pudding's just – Just normal.

James   There was fuckloads of meat – I mean look at all the leftovers. They'll be doing game pie for weeks off that.

Alistair   And we're happy with 'good enough', are we?

James   That was a fucking decent roast, it was –

Guy   It was a fucking decent roast, thank you.

Alistair   Get the landlord in, get him to explain himself.

George   Guys, let's not have a fight about –

Dimitri   I'm happy to speak to the guy if you want me to.

James   If that's what you want to do, fine.

Hugo   No no no no, it should be the president who complains.

Dimitri   Really, I can do it – Leighton clearly doesn't *care*.

Hugo   Doesn't have the gravitas if it isn't the president.

James   Guys, I *do* care, course I care. It's our night.

Alistair   Well is it or isn't it?

Hugo   If it's our night, we should get our way.

Guy   Oh god it's just a pile of meat.

Toby   Gauntlet's down, mate.

James   Fine – fine. Picking up the gauntlet. If that's what the evening needs.

Dimitri   Next time he comes in, yeah?

Ed   When they bring in the ten-cake cake.

James *salutes.*

James   For King and Country.

Hugo   Oh Captain my Captain!

James   *Brigadier,* thank you.

Dimitri   How about something to help you over the top?

James   What?

Dimitri   You know, get on the *snow patrol*.

Toby   Weaponise!

Harry   Drop the C-bomb.

Ed   What are they talking about?

Guy   *Coke*, you douche.

James   Yeah yeah – George?

George   Right, yeah, um. Yeah, about that –

James   What?

George   Yeah, um. Bit of a problem with the old, um, *procurement* actually.

Toby   Oh *what*?

James   It's your turn, mate –

George   Yeah, well I tried, OK. Managed to find this chap in the first year, yeah, who knows this chap he gets it off in Blackbird Leys but he said I had to get it myself,

Alistair   But you didn't get it?

George   Look I had to leave the beagling dinner early, yeah, which *really* isn't the done thing, then I had to wait on this bench for ages and it was bloody cold, all these people staring at me –

Dimitri   Mate, you didn't go to Blackbird Leys in your plus fours, did you?

Hugo   Foolhardy.

George   So this quite smelly gentleman comes up and starts chatting to me and I assume it's my chap because he looks like a drug dealer –

Dimitri   Drug dealers just look normal, mate.

George   Yes well I know that *now*, so –

So I'm really not sure of the protocol but eventually he cuts to the chase at which point I realise he's not the chap I'm supposed to meet, he's actually a sort of a sort of a –

Guy   Tramp.

George   You know, a homeless. So we're chatting and he –

Dimitri   Does this story have an end or just a middle?

George   I got mugged, OK?

Hugo   Oh mate.

George   Asks me if I've got any change. And I said. I said 'I'm really sorry, I've only got notes'.

Dimitri   'I've only got notes'? What did you expect?

George   Yes, OK, yes. Anyway, he pulls a knife and demands I give him my – My wallet.

Then the actual dealer actually turns up and yes, Dims, he did look perfectly normal, then when I told him I hadn't got the money anymore he looked very cross and did some shouting and then I did some running away.

Toby   Fuck.

Guy   No sniffy.

Hugo   Chaps, George got mugged.

Harry   Has anyone got some? Dims?

Dimitri   Riot Club's my night off from being powder-provider, mate.

Toby   What do we do, Leighton?

James   OK, guys, we'll just have to, um. Not.

Alistair   Oh this is fucked.

Harry   Hey, Balf – the farmers in the bar you were talking to?

George   Yeah?

Harry   Go and see if they've got any Ketamine or something.

George   What?

Harry   You know, for horses.

Hugo   Or we could stop behaving like –

Harry   Seriously Balf – go and get some Ket from the farmers.

George   They're not going to have any on them.

Harry   They might.

Guy   Go on, Balf.

George   No they won't because a) why would they bring horse tranquiliser to the pub and b) even if they did it'd be liquid cause you can't get a horse to snort something and 3) I don't see why we have to take drugs anyway, I don't even like it – coke doesn't even really do anything except make you feel rotten the next day I think I'd rather have a pint, actually.

The door opens and **Rachel** *comes in, carrying a tray.*

Seriously.

Rachel   Just come in to clear. Everything alright for you?

James   Yes. Fine, thank you.

She puts the tray down and starts to collect the main course plates onto it.

Dimitri   Leighton?

James   Yes, OK. Hi – Sorry, Rachel, isn't it?

Rachel   Yeah.

James   Is your dad around, Rachel?

Rachel   He's sorting out the Ruby Wedding. D'you need to speak to him?

James   No no, don't worry – I'll have a chat with him later.

Dimitri   Talk to Rachel about it.

Rachel   What?

James   I said I'd talk to Chris, not –

Miles   We can speak to you, since you're here, Rachel.

James   No, mate, I said I'd –

Harry   Rachel's our mate, you can talk to her.

Alistair   What have you got to say to the lady, *Brigadier*?

Rachel   Sorry, is there a problem?

James   Right, yeah. Yeah, the guys would like to complain about –

Dimitri   No, you – *you*'d like to complain.

James   OK, yeah. Sorry about this, know this isn't your fault, but we'd like to complain about the fact of the um, the ten bird roast, because it only had nine birds in it, actually. By our reckoning.

Rachel   Really? I told him you were all too pissed to notice.

James   Sorry?

Rachel   He was worried about it earlier, said the butcher let him down, couldn't get hold of any guinea fowl this week but didn't tell him till the last minute. I said I couldn't imagine anyone being bothered to count the rings on it.

James   No, well. I'm surrounded by pedants.

George   I'm not a peasant!

James   *Pedant*, not peasant.

George   I've got patent.

James   I know, I said *pedant*.

Hugo   Could have got a guinea fowl out of Harry's back garden.

Alistair   His back garden's most of Warwickshire.

Harry   Honestly – it's not *most of*.

James   It's just that when we arrange something, we kind of expect to get it, you know?

Dimitri   When we're paying for it.

Rachel   I'm sure he'll have tried to tell you about it.

James   He actually kind of didn't.

Rachel   OK, is anyone still hungry? Did anyone not have enough to eat?

'Cause I could make you an omelette?

Alistair   The thing is, Rachel, we're not your normal punters –

James   These chaps have eaten in some of the finest restaurants in the country.

Dimitri   The world, mate.

Rachel *laughs.*

Rachel   So what you doing in Kidsbury, then?

Oh yeah. Young Enterprise.

Rachel *picks up the tray.*

I'll tell Chris what you said.

She realises she can't get out of the door without putting the tray down again, but **James** *leaps up to open it for her.*

James   Other than the numbers issue, I mean what there was of it was lovely, so you know –

Rachel   Yeah. You might want to keep the noise down a bit.

Rachel *goes out.* **James** *shuts the door behind her and turns back to look at the table.*

George   Boo.

James *sits down.*

Guy   Well that could have gone better.

James   It's fine, it's fine.

Toby   Mate, you got rinsed.

James   No I didn't.

George   Chaps chaps, come on.

Toby   Leighton got totally fucking rinsed. 'Other than the numbers issue it was lovely' – what the fuck?

James   OK, fine.

James *stands up.*

Point of order: anyone fancy a dregsing?

Toby   What, now?

James   Suddenly in the mood for one.

Guy   Seconded!

Hugo   Do we have to?

Harry   Thirded!

Toby   Well fucking come on then, let's get it done.

Toby *stands up in preparation.*

OK, so once this is over you can't take the piss anymore, yeah?
Total fucking moratorium.

And no chewing gum, no jizz, Villiers –

James   Just a minute, Tubes. Sit down a sec.

Toby   What?

James *pulls a piece of paper out of his pocket.*

James   Something to read out first.

Toby   What, what is it?

James   Just something to put all this in context, that's all. For the
new boys.

James *reads:*

'Dear Mr. Bingham. I am writing to express my great regret for
recent events for which –

Toby *leaps from his chair, trying to grab the piece of paper from*
James, *but* **George** *and* **Dimitri** *jump up and pull him away.*

Harry   Oh mate.

Toby   That's private, that's a private –

James   Yeah, wasn't going to do it but you've pissed me off, so –

Toby   Fuck.

James   This is a letter Tubes wrote back in –

James *consults the letter.*

March this year. So shortly after the shitstorm.

Alistair   How'd you get it?

James   Just requested a copy for the archives.

Hugo   Get Tubes to read it.

Guy   Yeah, you read it.

Toby   Fuck's sake.

Ed   Go Tubes!

Harry   Don't let him grab it.

James   I'll hold it, yeah. You read – from there –

Toby   'On the night in question, myself and a number of other Riot Club members attended Spires, a nightclub in Oxford.

James   No, next bit, that bit

Toby   I took it upon myself to procure some female company for the party, and invited two young ladies to join us in the VIP area. One of whom was Clare Sweet'.

Harry   *Total* bitch.

Guy   What kind of a name is *Clare Sweet*?

Toby   Bit like *Lauren Small*, isn't it?

Hugo   Read, Tubes.

Toby   'I spent the next portion of the evening in private conversation with Ms Sweet, during which contravened club secrecy rules.

George   Boo!

Toby   I am also aware by report that I may have said some wrong-headed things which caused the club to seem ridiculous'.

Harry   What, like 'I love the sound of breaking glass'?

Miles   Oh my god, did he say that?

Dimitri   Yeah, then he held his glass out and dropped it on the floor.

Miles   Did it break?

Dimitri   Nope. Fell on a scarf.

The boys laugh.

Toby   'I had no idea that Ms Sweet had begun to record our conversation on a mobile phone. Nothing in Ms Sweet's demeanour –

Harry   Sorry, Tubes, I think someone's phone's ringing?

Guy   Oh, that's me, sorry, just got a new ringtone. . .

Guy *takes his phone out of his pocket – the ringtone is a sample of* **Toby**'s *voice over and over saying 'I love the sound of breaking glass' and 'Total carnage'.*

Toby   'I tried to take' – Fuck you, Bellingfield – 'I tried to take the audio clip off YouTube as soon as –

OK, there's another phone going –

Harry *pulls out his phone, playing a sample of* **Toby** *saying 'all the way to Chunderland' over a dance beat.*

It stops quite suddenly and Harry fiddles with the phone.

Wait – fuck – call me again, Dims.

Dimitri *does so.* **Harry**'s *phone rings again and the boys dance along to the ringtone for a moment.*

Toby   OK, whatever. Oxford Student, Daily Mail, picture of the Prime Minister, you know the rest.

James   Just want the guys to hear the final paragraph.

Toby   Jesus.

Guy   Take it to the bridge, Tubes.

Toby   'I know that I made a grave error of judgement and deeply regret that my actions have brought the club into disrepute.

Hugo   Oh god, I can't bear it

Toby   My error stemmed mostly from a feeling of pride at being a member of the club, which I struggled not to share. I have taken a long hard look at myself and have –

George   Oh no no no –

Toby   'Have suffered a number of sleepless nights thinking about –

Hugo   Oh god Leighton make it stop –

James   Move to a dregs?

Guy   Seconded.

Harry   Thirded.

Dimitri   Fourthed.

James   Gentlemen, please dregs your glasses.

The boys grab their half-full wine glasses.

George   God, I love a dregsing.

Miles   What do I do?

Alistair   Put something in your wine – snot, spit, whatever –

The boys individually adulterate their own glass of wine, variously adding snot, saliva, phlegm, salt and pepper, torn-up bread, earth from a nearby plant pot, ear wax, candle wax etc.

Harry *turns away from the table and unzips.*

Toby   Guys, clemency, please?

Harry   Thank fuck – I needed a piss anyway.

Hugo   Oh Villiers, put it away.

Toby   Mate please don't piss in it –

Harry   Oops I'm pissing in it.

Ed   I've just put a little bit of salt in mine, so –

James   Ready Tubes? One minute on the clock to get round the table.

Everyone done?

Miles   Hang on a sec –

Miles *finishes crumbling a piece of bread into his glass of wine, then looks around for something more.*

Wait a sec –

Miles *grabs a bowl of pot pourri from the sideboard and sprinkles some of it into his glass then stirs it with a spoon and sits back, satisfied.*

OK.

James   Toby – dregs!

The boys clap in time and shout 'dregs dregs dregs' as **Toby** *moves around the table, drinking down each dregsed glass of wine.*

After five glasses, **Toby** *clings to the back of the chair, doubled-over, nearly falling.*

Toby   Bag –

The boys hold out a bag for him which he vomits into.

Toby *pulls himself up again and continues around the table, drinking another two glasses, after which he falls onto his knees.*

Harry   Try and finish it, mate.

Toby *pulls himself up again and drinks one more glass. He falls to his knees again and holds out his hand for the next glass, but* **Alistair** *pulls it out of his reach.*

Alistair   No.

Toby   I can do it –

Alistair   No, mate –

Toby   Come on, want to get it done –

Alistair   Just – what are we doing?

What are we doing?

Dimitri   Don't suddenly get all Save The Children, Ryle.

Alistair   I'm not – I'm just – Hasn't he taken enough shit for this?

James   He has to be punished.

Alistair   For what? For being proud of the club? Why shouldn't he –

James   He *talked* about it.

Alistair   Didn't lie, did he? Now fucking look at him –

James   Sorry, what you saying, mate.

Alistair   I'm saying – I don't know – I'm saying – I mean isn't that exactly what they want?

People just waiting for us to put a foot wrong so they can take the piss, yeah? I mean doesn't it feel a bit like the world's queuing up to shit on us?

You know, the wrong wine, fucking gritty pate – sorry Bell-end but it was shit –

Guy   It wasn't shit –

Alistair   Leighton late for his own dinner because he's doing a maths test for a fucking *internship*? Jesus, when did that happen? Fucking *begging* for jobs.

James   We're not being shat on, not begging for jobs it's –

Harry*'s phone rings. Ten sets of ears prick up.*

Harry   Gentlemen – it's cock o'clock.

The boys whoop with joy.

Dimitri   Bring on the ladyfun.

Harry *answers the phone, motioning to the others to hush.*

Harry   Hello? Hi – are you here?

Ed   Tell her I've got my cock out ready for her.

Harry   He what? Oh fuck.

Dimitri   What's happening?

Harry   Landlord won't let her in.

Guy   What?

Toby   Fucksticks.

Alistair   Yeah, this is what I'm –

Harry   Where are you now?

Harry *goes to the window and looks out.*

OK, go round to the left – no, we're in a room round the back. No no, he won't know –

James   Is this a good idea?

Harry   Can you see me at the window – I'm waving at you – OK, yeah, come here –

Harry *opens the window.*

Toby   You going out?

Harry   No, she's coming in. *Harry leans out of the window.*

Hi!

A woman's face appears at the window.

Charlie   Hi. Harry?

Harry   Charlie, yeah?

Charlie *looks into the room and sees all the other boys.*

This is Charlie, chaps, she's a – what d'you say, 'call girl'?

Charlie   Um. Escort. Is this a stag party?

Harry   No no, god no. Come in.

Charlie   Um. Might have to give me a hand.

Harry   Pleasure. Is there a step on that –

Charlie   Yeah yeah.

Harry *gives* **Charlie** *his hand and she steps up to the window and swings one of her legs into the room.*

Dignified, isn't it?

Harry   Spot of bother in the bar?

Charlie   Old client of mine's sat in there, tipped off the landlord.

Usually meet somewhere a bit more discreet.

Charlie *brings her other leg through the window and faces the boys. She's wearing a demure(ish) black dress and heels. You'd have to be a seasoned punter to spot she was an escort.*

Harry   OK, well you're here now, so –

This is my friends – James –

Charlie   Hi.

James   Welcome.

Charlie *shakes* **James**' *hand, to the boys' surprise. She shakes hands with each of them as she's introduced.*

Harry   Alistair,

Alistair   Hi.

Harry   George,

George *giggles.*

Charlie   Hello.

Harry   Dimitri,

Dimitri   Charmed.

Harry   Guy, Toby – we call him Tubes –

Charlie   I won't ask why.

Harry   Ed – he'll probably dribble on you,

Charlie   Ahh.

Harry   Miles,

Miles   Hi.

Harry   Oh and Hugo, but he's gay, so –

Charlie   Shame – you look like a catch.

Hugo   Thanks.

Charlie *looks at* **Harry**.

Charlie   So, um –

Harry   Yeah. Here we are.

Dimitri   Would you like a drink?

Charlie   Maybe in a minute, thanks. (*To* **Harry**.) You've got a room, have you?

Harry   Yes. Here.

Charlie *looks around at the room.*

Charlie   This?

Harry   Yeah.

Charlie   OK, where are the others going to go?

Harry   Sorry?

Charlie   While we're seeing each other.

Harry   No no, they'll be here. What we were thinking was if you, um, were under the table, and all of us sitting around it, so –

Charlie   What am I doing under the table?

Harry   Um, us. One at a time.

Dimitri   Slightly more than one at a time, maybe, um –

Charlie   You're talking about oral? On all of you.

Miles   We'd give you a cushion.

Charlie   What?

Miles   You know, for your knees.

Hugo   Milo –

Charlie *laughs*.

Charlie   Yeah, um. I'm sorry, there's been crossed lines here somewhere.

Harry   Crossed lines?

Charlie   I do classic outcall – two hours, normal package. That's what I do. You seem to want more of a specialist thing.

Guy   What's the normal package?

Charlie   Straight sex or oral. Like a date, only I won't ring in the morning.

Any extras have to be agreed in advance.

Guy   What counts as extras?

Charlie   Well, if you wanted BDSM or water sports or whatever, they'd send a girl who specialises. I do a more classy sort of service. Conversation.

What did you say to the agency?

Harry   Just said I wanted to hire a girl, I mean they didn't say –

Charlie   Did they not tell you extras had to be agreed in advance?

Harry   Yeah, I just – I thought he was asking if I wanted more than one girl.

Dimitri   Villiers.

Harry   Well I don't know, they throw all these fucking euphemisms at you –

Dimitri   One would probably assume we pay you and you do whatever's required.

Charlie   The agency should have made it clear –

Harry   I've paid a deposit. Which I was given to believe is non-refundable.

Charlie   Yeah, you'll have to take that up with the agency.

Dimitri (*to* **Harry**)   You didn't think to check?

Toby   Schoolboy, mate.

Harry   Look, I'm sure we can work something out, can't we?

Charlie   What d'you mean?

Harry   A considerably bigger fee? Which the agency needn't know about.

Charlie   I'm a professional.

Harry   Yeah, course. Just it's an important night for us, and I –

Charlie   I don't do anything off the books.

Harry   No, OK, but you're here now, so –

These are special guys, Charlie and we're celebrating tonight.

I mean if you go away you don't earn the other half of the money, right?

Charlie   If you want to book a hotel room I'll happily go to it with you.

James *laughs.*

Harry   What, Leighton?

James   We're not allowed to leave the room.

Toby   There's no fucking point if we don't all get to do it.

Hugo   One for all and all for one.

Ed   What if we *all* left the room in turn?

Charlie I'm not going to do ten people in two hours.

Hugo Make it nine.

Charlie I don't do more than two visits in a row without a proper break.

Harry What break d'you need when you're just lying there? What?

Charlie I'm not just a live version of the sock you wank into.

Harry OK, I'm not just a fucking wallet.

Sorry, trying to be a gentleman here, but I'm actually really fucked off.

Charlie You can take it up with Paul at the office if you want to complain.

Harry I do want to complain. I've been misled.

Charlie Call him right now if you want.

Harry I will.

Charlie You got the number?

Harry Yes thank you.

Harry *takes out his mobile and dials the number, putting the phone to his ear.*

Ringing.

Hugo I know, why don't we leave it, try to keep a tiny scrap of dignity.

George *approaches* **Charlie**.

George Scuse me?

Charlie Hi.

George Don't you need the money?

Charlie Not especially.

George   OK. You don't need some drugs, or –

Toby   Balf –

Charlie   No I don't. Thank you.

George   So, why do you, um –

Charlie   I'm sorry?

George   Sorry, just wondering why you, you know –

Charlie   You want to finish that sentence?

George   No, I think I'll leave it.

James   I'm never going to have an erection again.

Harry   Fucking answer phone.

Harry hangs up.

Toby   Aren't you going to leave a message?

Harry   And say what?

Charlie   Must be on the other line. You'll have to call him later.

Dimitri   You don't think he'll be pissed off at you for losing a job?

Charlie   I don't have to do anything I don't want to. If I'm not 100% happy I can walk away.

Harry   Look. Charlie. Here's my problem. I've promised these boys they'll get a blowjob tonight – if you don't do it, I look like a cunt.

Charlie   You could do it yourself – you'll be under the table, a mouth's a mouth.

Harry   I'm not sure you quite appreciate who you're –

Charlie   I don't care who you are, it's –

Harry   Why can't you just do it?

Charlie   I think I've made it clear what I –

Harry   Why can't you buckle down and –

Charlie   What?

Harry   Fuck's sake you're a whore, aren't you?

The word hangs in the air.

Charlie   Right. I think I'm going now, aren't I?

Yeah.

James   D'you think you could exit through the window? Only we don't want the landlord –

Charlie   Whatever.

Charlie *steps up onto the chair by the window.*

Harry   No wait, wait, look Charlie I'm sorry, I didn't mean – we can work something out so everyone's –

Harry *grabs* **Charlie** *by the arm.*

Charlie   Hands off.

Alistair   Mate, step away. Let it go.

Harry *lets go of* **Charlie**'s *arm. She's about to start climbing out of the window when the door opens and* **Chris** *comes in.*

Chris   You – Out, please.

Charlie   Yeah, I'm going, I'm going.

Alistair   Mate, it's fine, she's gone.

Chris   This is a family restaurant.

Charlie   I'm going, aren't I?

James   It's alright, she's going.

Charlie (*to* **Miles**)   Hand, please.

Chris   I won't have it, I've asked you nicely –

Miles *gives her his hand to help her out of the window.*

Charlie   Shut up, I'm fucking going, OK?

Chris   Yes, well I'll be a lot happier once you've gone.

Charlie   I've gone I've gone. Jesus.

Charlie, *having climbed out of the window, disappears across the car park.*

Chris *looks at the boys.*

Dimitri   I'm so sorry, is there a problem?

Chris   Yes, actually. Yes. I'm sorry, but I'm trying to run a family restaurant here.

George   Gastropub.

James   Listen, I just want to say –

Chris   Look, you might like that sort of thing, I find it extremely offensive.

Some of the lads from the village wanted a strippergram in here last year and I wouldn't let them – can't have one rule for them and another for you – notwithstanding that it's against the law, what she –

Dimitri   We're friends, aren't we? Let's not get into the legality issue.

Chris   I think it's time you left, please.

George, **James** *and* **Guy** *head towards* **Chris**, *turning up the charm.*

George   Oh no, please, come on –

James   Really, we're everso sorry, can't we –

Guy   Thing is, most of us went to boarding school, we're not very good at –

Chris   The Ruby Wedding table – who by the way are sat just the other side of that wall – threatening to leave if I don't turf you out, can't take the noise any more.

James   I'm so sorry, we really didn't realise –

Guy   You know what boys are like –

Dimitri   It's our AGM, you see, so –

Chris   I'd like you to leave. I don't want to get the police involved.

*The other boys scramble towards **Chris**, trying to help placate him. **Alistair** stays where he is.*

Harry   The police? Hang on, let's –

Hugo   I'm sure we don't need to bother the police with –

Toby   Fucking grow a pair.

Hugo   Tubes –

Guy   Honestly, we're just idiots, so –

Chris   When it's upsetting my other customers –

Alistair   How much is the bill?

The others fall quiet.

Chris   Sorry?

Alistair   How much is the bill for the Ruby Wedding?

Chris   What's that got to –

Alistair   We're spending what tonight –

James   Al –

Alistair   We're spending what tonight?

James   'Bout three and a half grand.

Alistair   Three and a half thousand pounds. And the Ruby Wedding bill comes to what – how many of them?

Chris   Eight, but that's not –

Alistair   Eight people off the set menu, six bottles of wine, fifteen percent tip, I mean we're talking a few hundred, aren't we?

Aren't we?

Surely the question is – Is which of these two parties can you least afford to lose?

James   Ryle, don't –

Alistair   Let the man speak.

Chris   It's not about the money, it's about goodwill, these are my customers –

Alistair   Exactly – what kind of customers do you want: hundreds or thousands?

Alistair *pauses for a moment to let* **Chris** *think.*

I tell you what. What say we pay the bill for the Ruby Wedding table? Gesture of *goodwill*.

Alistair *turns to the others: 'who's got the money?'*

Right, chaps?

Dimitri *reaches into his jacket pocket and pulls out a wad of cash.*

Dimitri   What was it, three hundred pounds? Four?

Dimitri *counts out the money.*

Alistair   Make it five.

Dimitri   Bottle of champagne as well.

Dimitri *holds the money towards* **Chris**.

Alistair   We might not be to your *taste*, but we always pay our way.

Chris *looks at the money.*

We wouldn't want you to be out of pocket.

Chris *takes the money.*

Chris   Well. I'll see if they're happy with that.

Alistair   Please do.

Chris   This is what they teach you at boarding school, is it?

Alistair   Do send them our congratulations.

Chris *moves towards the door.* **James** *and* **Guy** *follow him.*

James   I'm very sorry – we're very sorry.

Guy   You see we don't get together very often, so when we see each other we get a bit over-excited.

Toby   What about pudding?

Ed   Yay pudding!

Alistair   Send the girl in with the pudding. We'll be fine.

James   The food's been excellent. Really.

Guy   Friends again, yes?

Chris   Just keep it down, please.

James   You won't hear another squeak out of us, really.

George   Thank you!

Chris   Desserts'll be along in a minute. *Gentlemen.*

Chris *leaves.* **James** *closes the door.*

Alistair   What a fucking. Knob-jockey.

All eyes turn to **Alistair**.

James   Mate – he'll –

Alistair   I don't care if he hears me.

Dimitri   Fucking liberty.

Alistair   You see what I mean?

James   Come on, Al, he was –

Alistair   Taking the piss, mate.

Toby   Taking the fucking piss.

Hugo   'Is this what they teach you at boarding school?'

James   We did try to get a prozzer through a – didn't chuck us out, did he?

At least he was willing to –

Alistair   Snide remarks with one hand, but he's still taking the money with the other, isn't he? Still taking the fucking money.

Harry   'I'll see if they're happy with that'.

Ed   *Total* dickwad.

James   You offered him a deal, he took it, what's the –

Alistair   Yeah, but he keeps the moral high ground. Cause god forbid he gives that up. What about *not* take the money if you feel that fucking strongly? Or what about take the money and shut the fuck up?

Toby   As if.

Alistair   I mean who the fuck does he – Does he think he's some kind of *lord* cause he's got a gastropub? What, thin beef and gay puddings for people who think cause they're eating orange fish it must be smoked salmon?

Harry   Gaylord.

Alistair   Calling us 'Gentlemen' as if he had any idea, any *idea* of what the word means. Graciously letting us stay if we don't smoke or call a prozzer or make any noise – what is this, the fucking Quiet Carriage?

Toby   Yeah! I mean *boo*.

Alistair   I mean just cause he's got Farrow and Ball on the – what colour is that, *kidney*? – he reckons it gives him the right to sneer at us 'cause he's what, honest, decent, hardworking? He thinks he's earned it. He also thinks Rugby League is a sport. I mean this man keeps cheese in the fucking *fridge*.

Hugo   Which he should hang for, frankly.

Alistair   'While you're under my roof you respect my rules'? I've got a new rule for you, mate, it's called survival of the fittest, it's called 'fuck you – we're the Riot Club'. Respect that. 'Can't have one rule for them and another rule for you' – why not? Seriously, why the fuck not? We're the fucking Riot Club. And we've hardly started, mate.

And *her*, stuck up bitch, fucking skank – you're a prostitute, love, get on your knees. 'Not doing that, it's not in my job description', 'I'm a professional, ring my line manager' – I'll wring your fucking neck if you're not careful. What, you're too good for us? We've got the finest sperm in the country in this room, she should be paying *us* to let her drink it.

Harry   Fuck yeah. Girls queuing round the block.

Alistair   And these people think *we're* twats. Are we going to sit here and take it, carry on taking it? Tonight of all nights?

Guy   The pate tasted like jizz. There, I've said it.

Harry   It fucking did.

Alistair   This bourgeois outrage when we do anything, say *anything*. Lurking round every corner, trying to smoke us out. Anything we ever build or achieve, anything with the slightest whiff of magnificence – who the fuck are these people? How did they get *everywhere*, how did they make everything so fucking second-rate?

Thinking they're cultured cause they read a big newspaper and eat asparagus and pretend not to be racist. Bursting a vein at the thought there's another floor their lift doesn't go up to, for all their *striving*. Honest, decent people hell-bent on turning this country to fuck.

'You're not allowed to do that', 'You can't have that, that's not fair'. You know what's not fair? That we have to even listen to them. Thinking cause there's more of them, they're better when they're worth their weight in shit – that's not sweat on their palms, it's *envy*, it's resentment and it stinks like a fucking *drain* – I mean I am sick, I am sick to fucking death of *poor people*.

Interval.

Act Two

Scene One

The boys are eating pudding, faces close to large dishes of Eton Mess.

Ed   So my mother and father are stuck in this tiny little sitting room upstairs, huddled round a gas fire, rooms all round them getting opened to visitors cause they've got some cunting tapestry or William of Orange slept there. Next time I go back they'll have stuck my parents in the fucking Buttery.

Harry   Same at mine, mate.

Ed   Held to ransom by the National Trust.

Harry   Board of Trustees.

Ed   Guides walking through the house saying 'we restored this room last year' as if it's *theirs*.

Alistair   Shameful.

Harry   Last time I was home this guide woman – I think she must have been new – she told me I couldn't go behind one of the ropes. I said yes I can it's my house.

Ed   Fucking sick of it.

Toby   The *fucking. Wankers*.

Toby *drinks.*

George   Haven't people always wanted a look inside big houses? We've always had visitors.

Hugo   They're not visitors now, they're *customers*.

Harry   Every year it's thinking of new ways to get the punters in. Used to be just the summer, now they've got this German Christmas craft fair.

Ed   Yeah, we're having that. Shitty wooden toys.

Harry   Whole place smells of cinnamon.

Ed   We're having Husky races this year.

Harry   And *endless* film crews, fucking Jane Austen.

Hugo   *Sex and Sexibility*.

Ed   We've got to reschedule my sister's wedding because it clashes with the teddy bears' picnic and they've already done the leaflets.

It's so *grubby*.

Alistair   Yeah, exactly – we're all bending over backwards.

Miles   It's all about bears with you, isn't it?

Hugo   The age of compromise . . .

Ed   It's an important collection.

James   It's good, isn't it, if they want to visit? What history's for.

Hugo   No, because – no, Leighton, it's not *their* history. These are – these are private houses, family *homes*. And they were built by people who knew how to actually *live*, people with a bit of –

I mean men who built things *big*, so big you look at them now and think god, how many people did that take to –

And lived *unapologetically*, that's the thing. Defended themselves if they needed to, I mean they wrote the history of this country in their own *blood*. Built these houses as proof of their, their *magnificence* because they were proud of who they were and what they stood for.

Now they're trampled through by people only there for the cream tea and the novelty thimble.

Harry   Except they don't want the cream tea anymore, reckon the buns are 'too expensive'. Everything's about *value for money,* grubby little voucher schemes.

Guy   Fucking recession, isn't it?

Alistair   Happening before the recession, mate. Blair's lot, giving the kids too much pocket money,

Harry   'Because you're worth it'.

Dimitri   Yawn.

Hugo (*turning to* **James**)   Why should Ed's family have to put up with their house getting turned into a theme park?

James   Because otherwise they couldn't afford to get the roof fixed.

George   Always the roof.

Ed   Roof wouldn't be a problem if they hadn't taken all the money when grandpa died.

James   Yeah, OK, but you know, your parents made a decision, didn't they, to open the –

George   Our roof's got holes you could fire a cow through.

Dimitri   Bored of the roof now!

James   I'm just saying your family benefited from –

Harry   Yeah, till they stopped coming.

Alistair   And we know why they stopped, don't we? Cause they spent all the money on all this shiny new shit – massive fuckoff plasma-screen telly. Don't understand why they're not just born with it, why it doesn't just get handed to them –

James   OK, sure, 'mistakes were made', but our lot us are in power now, so –

Guy   True dat.

Alistair   We're not in power.

Guy   They'll get a majority next time, my uncle says –

Alistair   Does it *feel* like we're in power? Or does it feel like that fucking landlord, like people like him still get to shit wherever they want and we're just trailing round with a poop scoop?

Dimitri   Come on guys, who run the world?

Alistair   Not us. Clearly.

These people have gashed it up for us. We're all going to come out of college –

Harry   Which we worked fucking hard for, don't forget –

Alistair   Yeah, and there's going to be no jobs for us because of people like him.

Toby   I mean these people – *these people* –

James   OK fine. Everyone's suffering.

Ed   My brother's been made redundant.

Harry   Monters?

James   Where was he, Merrill?

Ed   Goldman.

George   But your brother's a legend.

Ed   Legend as in used to have a job, now doesn't.

Dimitri   He was only there five minutes.

Ed   Last in, first out, isn't it?

Dimitri   Shit.

Ed   No, I mean, he's *OK*. Says he going to buy an Airstream – one of those big old silver caravan things? Start a business doing street food at festivals and shit.

You know, *really* good burgers?

The boys think about this for a moment.

Alistair   I mean, *fuck*.

Guy   The fucking landlord.

Harry   We should totally do something to fuck him up.

Toby   The trouble is, right, the trouble is that these people –
they've got no fucking – I mean, have they? What a load of
fucking – fuck it makes me angry –

James   I just don't understand how you're pinning Monters'
redundancy on the landlord of this pub.

Harry   He took our prozzer away, we should get him back.

Alistair   Not just *him*, people like him.

Guy   Get the daughter back in.

Alistair   I mean, when you trace it back, yeah?

Toby   What I mean is – 'scuse me –

Toby *starts to ramble incoherently, a few phrases audible here and
there.*

James   Yeah, just a bit of a *hardline* position, isn't –

Alistair   OK. Fuck. Let's join it up, shall we?

So, OK, they want all the *stuff*, 95% mortgage, whatever, so they
all borrow more money than they can ever afford to pay back.

Toby   And that cunt of a girl going all 'Oh Toby' –

Alistair   They're obsessed with upward mobility but they're not
prepared to put the work in, it's all credit cards.

Toby   And then I fucking said –

Alistair   Then when the great New Labour shop in the sky goes
up in flames cause it turns out there *isn't* an endless supply of toys
and sweets, there can't be –

Toby   . . . should have gone Christ Church . . .

Alistair   They vote *us* back in to sort it all out, make it all go away.

James   Yeah, OK, cause we're good at solving –

Alistair   Haven't finished. But then they're all –

Toby   Because I've got the *right*, right –

Alistair   But then they're all like 'oh no, but don't do it like that', they don't –

Toby   My *human rights* –

Alistair   Fuck's sake, I'm trying to – someone put Tubes to bed, yeah?

Ed   Yeah yeah. Mate?

Toby   Hello.

Ed   Alright mate – how about a little sleep?

Toby *bangs his fist on the table, nearly upsetting his pudding bowl.*

Toby   No sleeping at the table!

James   Yeah, put him on the window seat or something.

Ed   Come on, mate, let's go and have a sit by the window.

Toby   OK.

Ed *leads* **Toby** *over to the window seat,* **Toby** *still muttering to himself.*

Ed   Nice bit of Bedfordshire.

Alistair   So they call us in –

Toby   The Duke of Bedfordshire!

Toby *stumbles and falls, stopping* **Alistair**.

Alistair   Jesus.

Harry *and* **Miles** *stand up to help* **Ed**.

Harry   That's it, mate.

Ed   Come on, sleepy-byes, OK?

Toby   OK. Love you.

Harry *and* **Miles** *get* **Toby** *to the window and help to settle him on the seat.* **George** *puts his hand up.*

George   Uh, guys, while we're *paused* – does anyone not want their pudding?

Toby *puts his head down on the windowsill in front of him and goes to sleep.*

Guy   Have Toby's one.

Ed, **Harry** *and* **Miles** *make their way back to the table.*

George   Super – chuck it over.

The pudding is passed over to **George**.

Yummy.

Sorry Ryle, you were saying – there's a sweet shop –

Alistair   No, they call us in to sort it out cause yes, we're good at that. But they don't want to give up the big house and the massive telly, cause now they've got used to the idea that they're worth it.

It's an impossible job, they've fucked us in every hole so I mean in what sense are we in power, Leighton?

Dimitri   OK, looking a lot like a conversation about politics here, can I just say?

Guy   State of the world, mate. Everything's political.

Dimitri   I'm here for the wine and the jokes.

Guy   Cause you've got no heritage, that's why.

Dimitri   I've got a boatload of –

Guy   No, mate, you've got a boat.

George   He's right, should be scrunching for talking about politics –

Alistair It's not your fault you can't see it, mate. People get used to being shat on, don't they?

James Oh come on, for fuck's sake – we're not being –

Alistair Seriously, mate. 'Them and us' all over again.

George No no no, it's not it's not at all. It's not them and us.

You know, at home, we're all suffering – my family, the people who work on the estate, the chaps in the village, in the pub, yeah? We've got a responsibility to help each other. And, you know, they look to people like us, to guide them, to –

Alistair They don't want to be *guided*.

George Yes they do.

Alistair They don't like us.

Guy They hate us.

George I just had a very nice drink with –

Alistair Who bought the drinks?

George Sorry?

Alistair Who paid for the drinks?

George I did.

Alistair Yeah. You think Farmer Barleymow and his mates aren't laughing at you out there right now? Dr Doolittle could talk to the animals, it didn't mean they wanted to be mates with him.

George, *they hate you.*

George *looks down at the table, takes a drink.*

Miles Haven't we just got to find a way to co-exist? With people who are different.

I mean when I was in Malawi, right, there were people who had *nothing*, literally nothing, and they didn't –

Alistair I'm not talking about proper poor people, like Africa or whatever.

Dimitri   Bored of Africa!

Hugo   What about Brixton?

Miles   What? Shut up.

Alistair   What's this?

Miles   It's got nothing to do with it.

Hugo   You had four stitches.

Miles   Mate –

Hugo   Miles got attacked. Brixton one night.

Harry   What were you doing in Brixton?

Miles   Went to a gig. People get mugged, it doesn't mean –

Hugo   I don't think it was a group of disgruntled Wykehamists.

Miles   It wasn't cause of being –

Hugo   What, you think they can't tell? You think you *blend in*?

It's not like they're trying to co-exist with us, is it?

Guy   How did it all get so shit?

Ed   The bloody landlord!

Alistair   No, mate. It's us. We let it happen.

Ed   Did we?

Alistair   We apologised. We *apologise* for being who we are, appropriate their values, pretend we agree with their fucking prudish –

Like Leighton, hanging out the back of that landlord all night – 'I'm so everso sorry' –

Guy   Yeah, 'you won't hear another squeak out of us'.

James   Mate –

Alistair   We do it to ourselves, yeah – all this shit about respecting other people's cultures – what, nicking trainers cause you can't be arsed to get a job and then calling it legitimate social protest? Fuck off.

How about you respect *my* culture?

James   Well, OK, because –

Alistair   Cause it's only going to get worse. More discontent, more *legitimate* protest.

Dimitri   Fuck, can somebody pass me that sword so I can stab my ears off?

Yeah fine, the country's gone to shit – d'you know what I think we should do? Get out of town for the night, get wasted.

Dimitri *stands up.*

Have a look under your placemats, chaps – little something for each of you.

The boys lift up their placemats and pull out an unfamiliar looking bank note, which they examine.

You know, what's this club *for*? What are we doing getting all misty about how hard done by we are? Let's fuck off somewhere, take copious party drugs, drink ourselves to oblivion and raise merry hell.

Miles   One Thousand. (*reading*) Eitt Pusund Kronur.

Guy   Eat poos and what?

Dimitri   Icelandic. We're going to Reykjavik.

Alistair   Iceland.

Dimitri   Gather ye rosebuds, mate.

Ed   Reykjavik.

Guy   What are we doing, fiscal irresponsibility tour?

Dimitri   It's an all-night party city. I've been.

Alistair   Persuade them into the Euro?

James We're going tonight?

Dimitri Yes, come on!

One thousand kronur – that's about a fiver in Icelandic money – not very much, but take it as a provocation, see how many vodkas you can get for it. And this –

He pulls out a wad of English money and flamboyantly attaches it to the table with **Lord Riot**'s *sabre.*

Is for the first man to piss on an ice sculpture.

Silence.

George Wouldn't that just make it melt?

Dimitri Chaps, what's wrong with you? Come on.

Guy I don't know, mate. All looks a bit flashy.

Dimitri Predictable response from Bell-end.

Alistair D'you really think that'll solve it?

Dimitri I'm not being –

Hugo Waving money about again, Dims.

Guy All he's got left, isn't it?

Hugo Fiddling while Athens burns.

Guy Cause he hasn't got a country anymore, so –

Dimitri I'm a British Citizen.

Guy Wearing a cravat doesn't make you British, mate.

This Mr Toad shit – who the fuck are you fooling?

Dimitri Fuck you, Bellingfield. Come on, chaps.

Toby *emits a strangled moan and twitches slightly.*

Toby Wuuuugh

The others notice but carry on.

Alistair   Dims, the trouble with going to Iceland is we'd have to come back.

Another noise from **Toby**, *whose body suddenly twitches and writhes.*

Toby   Mnnnnngh

Alistair   Fuck's sake, Tubes.

Hugo   You OK, Maitland?

George   Better out than in, mate.

Toby *stands up and staggers backwards into the room, still facing the window.*

Miles   Whoa, careful mate –

Hugo   Tubes, what you –

Toby *turns around to face the boys. But it's not* **Toby** *anymore.*

The boys sit up in fright.

Toby *appears to have morphed into an eighteenth century libertine. His voice comes out a little strangled at first, but commanding.*

Lord Riot   Gentlemen!

He looks around at the boys. Those at the end of the table nearest to him make a dash for the other end, cowering behind **James**.

Gentlemen of the Riot Club!

Why suffer ye this plague of peasants? Ye stand there wronged yet unequal to a fight – where are your wigs, men?

Ed   Where the fuck is Toby?

James   Maitland, stop being a –

Hugo   Mate, look at him – *it's not Maitland.*

Dimitri   What the fuck?

Hugo   I think it's Lord Riot.

Guy   I think we're supposed to speak to it.

Lord Riot   *It?*

Guy   Him, sorry, him.

James   Hugo?

Hugo   Why me?

George   He might do verse.

Hugo   Right, alright. Um. Are you. Lord Riot?

Lord Riot   Ye should know me by now.

Hugo   No, yes, of course. My lord.

Lord Riot   What appalling inaction is this? I find ye sitting like ladies at a bun shop, consumed by petty skirmishes.

Hugo   Yes. Yes, sorry about that.

Lord Riot   Do not weep into your syllabub, boys, with tales of how the world has bruised you. Is this the purpose for which my club was founded? A licking of wounds?

Hugo   No, um, probably –

Lord Riot   Leave off *quacking* and listen.

Hugo   Right. Sorry.

Lord Riot   I have been at every dinner since the club's inception, whether or not my presence was remarked. Rarely have I had great enough cause to intervene and it pains me to do so now, but intervene I must.

James   Um, should we be sitting down?

Lord Riot   Why must you brawl among yourselves? Ye are the finest of men, of all men – your fight is not with each other.

I know you feel your country running away from you, intent on mediocrity, garbling every morsel of magnificence into an inglorious gruel.

But we have seen worse, boys, we have seen worse, and without *whining*. When our French cousins were guillotined, did *we* weep into our pudding or did we stand our ground? Under your last queen, when legions of oily industrialists built machines they thought would make us obsolete, did we not show them *our* mettle?

Ninety years since, when the common man downed tools in peevish discontent, your counterparts stepped into the breach, uncomplaining. Drove omnibuses! Succeeded in putting the country back on its feet in but nine days.

The landlords of this world have thrown every kind of ordure at us down the years – are we not *still here*? Do you think I would let these merchants and hustlers quench my every fire with scorn and outrage? Are they the masters now, and you the servants?

Aye, boys, your times are bleak, but let them not divide you. You are the brightest, the boldest, the best. You think the true purpose of the club is simply the making of merriment? A place in which you *hide*? Never! The world wants you, boys – though it may not yet know it – it wants you, and it wants you to *lead*.

Alistair   OK, so what should we do?

Lord Riot   If you do not like what they have built, tear it down. Where is your wit, where your imagination? Tear it down and build something better – they will thank you in the end.

Alistair   Right, so how do we –

There's a knock at the door, at which **Lord Riot** *freezes, then droops, deflates.*

Hugo   Shit.

The door opens a crack.

Alistair   Wait!

The boys cluster around **Lord Riot**. **Rachel** *comes in.*

Harry   Shit – fuck –

Alistair   I said wait –

The boys try to hide **Lord Riot** *behind them, masking* **Rachel***'s view.*

Harry   Rachel! Why-eye!

Rachel   Um. Yes. Howay the lads.

Sorry, I need to clear the –

James   Yes, lovely, thank you.

Rachel   What have you –

Who've you got –

Harry   Who've we what?

James *gestures to the table.*

James   Please, go ahead and –

Rachel   Have you got someone behind –

James   What? No, nothing –

Rachel   You've got that woman, haven't you, look, you can't bring a –

Rachel *heads confidently towards the cluster of boys.*

Harry   No no no, it's –

Toby   Wuugh the fuck are you –

On hearing **Toby***'s voice, the boys move back from him, in relief.*

Harry   No, it's just Toby, see.

Ed   Toby!

James   Fuck, thank fuck.

Toby   Did you just touch my Jonty?

Alistair (*to* **Rachel**)   Just Toby, look.

Rachel   Right. Sorry, I thought –

Dimitri   Tubes, mate – you alright?

Toby   Fuck I'm gunna chunder . . . .

No I'm not.

Guy   OK, have a sit down, mate.

They lead **Toby** *to sit down in the nearest chair.*

Rachel   What's wrong with him?

Toby   My mouth tastes like –

Ed   Just a bit tired. Lots of essays.

Toby   Did I eat a *fox*?

James   Tuck him in, yeah.

(*To* **Rachel**.) Please, go ahead and clear.

Alistair *and* **Harry** *tuck* **Toby***'s chair closer into the table and he puts his head down on his hands.*

Rachel *puts her tray on a small service table at the side of the room, then moves to the table to start collecting the pudding dishes.*

Alistair (*to* **Harry**)   Mate, what about –

Alistair *nods towards* **Rachel**. **Harry** *nods back, understanding.*

Harry   Yeah, cool.

Guy   Rachel, can I just say that was the messiest Eton Mess I ever had. And I went to Eton.

Rachel   Good.

Alistair   Rachel?

Rachel   Hi.

Alistair   Hi. How'd you like to earn an extra £300 tonight?

Rachel   What?

Alistair *and* **Harry** *laugh. The laugh passes around the table as the other boys cotton on.*

Alistair   OK, here's what the thing is – we had this friend, this lady friend – well, as you know – who was supposed to be here with us right now, but actually – whoops – your dad's sent her away, so –

Rachel   Right.

Alistair   So we wondered if you might like to step in.

Ed   Oh my god, did he just ask that?

Rachel   Me?

Alistair   Pretty easy way to make £300.

Rachel   Are you asking what I think you're asking?

Alistair   No! God no.

Only blowjobs.

Guy   Under the table.

Ed   Yeah, you'd be under the table so you wouldn't have to see who you're –

Miles   Head-down Harriet.

Ed   Subtable Susan.

Alistair   Simple transaction – professional basis.

Rachel   I'll leave it, thank you.

Alistair   No, fine. Very modern.

Alistair *laughs.*

Miles   We're just joking, Rachel.

Rachel   OK.

Ed   Don't be offended, it's just jokes, yeah?

Alistair   Just a bit over-excited.

Rachel   Right, OK.

Harry   I'm sorry, Rachel.

Rachel   OK.

Ed   Sorry.

They subside a little. **Harry** *and* **Alistair** *look at each other.*

Harry *bangs his hand on the table.*

Harry   Chelsea Trots!

George   Hurrah.

Dimitri   Fuck's sake.

Harry (*to* **Dimitri**)   Mate – forfeits, yeah?

Ed   What?

Harry (*pointing at* **Rachel**)   Forfeits.

Ed   Oh OK, yeah.

Alistair   Places!

The boys start to move into place, spreading out around the table.

Alistair *looks at* **Miles**. **Miles** *looks at* **Rachel**.

Miles   D'you um, want to play, Rachel?

Harry   Quick game of the Chelsea Trots?

Rachel   I don't know what that is.

Guy   You must do, everyone does.

The boys move the chairs back from the table to give them more room.

Harry   Balf – you explain it to Rachel, yeah?

George is from a long line of champion Trotters.

George   Basically what happens is everyone dances round the circle and when the music stops you sit down only there's one chair too few, so –

Rachel   Musical Chairs.

George   If you like.

Guy   We playing Banbury Rules or Standard?

Alistair   Banbury, I think. Balf?

George   Yeah, Banbury. So you go round, right, and when the music stops –

Rachel   What are you going to play the music on?

George   Sorry?

Rachel   Did you ask for a CD player?

George   Oh no, there's isn't any music.

Rachel   You said 'when the music stops'.

George   Yeah, you just know when it stops.

Guy   It's usually quite obvious.

Rachel   I think I'll sit this one out.

The boys roll the bottom of their trousers up.

Alistair   Oh boo. Really?

Harry   OK, you'll have to just go round Rachel, OK, cause she's still clearing, so when you get to her, just go right round, like this, OK?

Alistair   Ready?

Hugo   Chair!

They move one chair so it's against the wall by the door. They all stand ready, facing clockwise. **Alistair** *looks at* **Rachel**.

Alistair   Here we go.

A look goes round the group, with coded gestures pointing at **Rachel**.

George   Wait for it – Standpipe!

Ed *nearly starts going round, then stops.*

Think about it . . . .

Bandicoot!

For some reason this is the right word, and the boys start to dance around the circle, wild and exuberant.

Rachel *continues to try to clear the plates from the table, trying not to look at the boys and laugh. Each time one of them gets to her he makes a big thing of going around her.*

James   New boys should be going in the opposite direction.

Miles   OK.

Miles *turns and dance in the opposite direction.* **Ed** *is already doing so.*

(*To* **Ed**.) You played this at school, right?

Ed   Yeah, didn't you?

Dimitri   This is so much better after a sniffy.

Exactly in unison, the boys suddenly all stop dancing and make a dash for the nearest chair.

James *is the only one who doesn't find a chair in time.*

Guy   Forfeit Leighton!

James   OK, and my forfeit is –

George   President can't decide his own forfeit.

James   Ryle, you want to nominate?

Alistair   OK, your forfeit, should you choose to accept it –

Harry   You have to accept it.

Alistair   Is to drink a bottle down in one!

James *glances at* **Rachel**.

James   What, don't I get – I thought we were doing –

Alistair   Warm-up round.

James Fuck, OK.

Harry Bottle for Leighton-Masters.

James *climbs onto a chair and a full bottle of wine is handed to him. He drinks half of it while the others cheer, but has to stop and take a breath. He staggers.*

Even **Rachel** *stops her clearing-up to watch.*

Alistair Come on, Leighton.

George Don't give up, mate, come on.

He downs the rest of the bottle and looks very much as if he'll vomit on the spot, but in fact doesn't.

He holds the bottle high and the boys cheer.

Off we go!

The boys dance around the circle, as before, and at the same moment, all dash for chairs.

This time it's **Miles** *who doesn't get one.*

Miles Ah, bollocks.

George And it's Mr Miley Milo Richards for the forfeit.

Harry Take it like a man, Milo.

George Forfeit, Ryle?

Alistair Aaaand, your forfeit is. . . . . You have to kiss Rachel.

Rachel What? No no.

Hugo You can't do sexual forfeits.

Alistair Forfeits are freestyle. Banbury Rules.

Rachel *makes for the door with a pile of dishes in her hand.*

Harry No no no, don't go. Don't go.

Rachel I've got to get back to the kitchen.

Guy Play the game, Rachel.

Rachel   I said I'm not playing.

Someone takes the pile of dishes from her. **Rachel** *is edged back into the room, away from the door.*

Alistair   If you're in the room, you're playing the game.

Harry   Just a kiss.

Rachel   I don't want to.

Hugo   Don't make him –

Guy   What, is it not in your job description?

Dimitri   You can't turn down a forfeit, Rachel, it's disrespectful to our culture.

Ed   We'll feel disrespected.

Hugo   Don't make Milo kiss her, come on.

Rachel   Sorry, I'm not –

Dimitri   What about a blow job, then?

Rachel   No way.

The boys laugh.

Dimitri   Rachel. The man's a thoroughbred.

Guy   Best sperm in the country – you should be thanking us.

Dimitri   Just have to kneel down and shut your eyes.

Alistair   Guys, guys, she doesn't have to give him a blojo.

Rachel *makes a move towards the door.*

You just have to kiss him.

Miles   Wait, Rachel, Rachel. Don't you want to, even a bit? Come on.

Hugo   Miles –

Rachel   No, I. No.

Alistair   Have you got a boyfriend, Rachel, is that it?

Rachel   Yes. Actually.

Alistair   Nice, is he?

Rachel   Yes. He is.

Alistair   Treats you nice. Takes you out – cinema, nice Italian,

Dimitri   Probably splits the bill.

Alistair   D'you split the bill, Rachel? Bet you split the bill.

You telling me you wouldn't trade up if you had the chance?

Miles *steps forward and without warning grabs* **Rachel** *and kisses her on the mouth. He holds her firmly in his arms so that she struggles, but can't get free of him.*

Eventually **Rachel** *manages to pull away, and turns to try to get to the door, but there are too many boys in the way for her to push through.*

Hugo   Let her out.

Rachel   Let me out.

Harry   Didn't you like it?

A strangled noise comes from **Toby***. He sits up, his body heaving. The others notice at once.*

Ed   Tubes?

Guy   Fuck, is he going again?

The others gather around him, concerned, clearing the way to the door.

Toby   No, fine, I'm fine.

Rachel *dashes out.* **Harry** *notices and takes a step towards the door, but* **Alistair** *stops him.*

Alistair   Let her go – bigger fish, yeah?

Ed   Chaps, don't crowd him.

Toby *runs his hands through his hair, knocking the wig off without realising.*

Hugo (*to* **Miles**) What the fuck was that?

Miles I'm not your rent boy.

Hugo Yeah, I got that.

Toby (*He looks around*) Are we still being sad?

Alistair No, mate – we're just getting going.

Toby Awesome. I am the trashmeister.

Alistair Let's do this!

Ed You want to give the pins a go, mate?

Toby *stands up – he's a little wobbly, then regains his balance.*

Toby Whoa – there we go. Back in the snaddle.

Harry Sabrage!

Alistair Erect the barricade!

Dimitri *grabs a chair and puts it under the door handle.*

Guy Quick – quick – get the champagne.

Dimitri Barricade erect, my lord.

George God I love this.

Alistair *climbs up to stand on the table.*

Guy Champagne!

Alistair Everyone feeling frisky?

A bottle of champagne is handed to **Alistair**.

And the sword.

Guy Sword!

Harry *hands* **Alistair** *the sabre.*

Alistair Never let it be said we don't take our work seriously, chaps.

Alistair *turns to* **James**, *holding the champagne and the sabre towards him.*

Sorry, should you be –

James   No mate, you do it.

Alistair   Gentlemen – for what we're about to do, may the good Lord Riot make us truly trashful. Let's make this one extra spicy.

Alistair *holds the champagne in front of him, swiping the sword along the neck of the bottle.*

All   HO!

The cork flies off and champagne sprays everywhere. The club roars.

They set to work trashing the room: it's orchestrated and rhythmic, almost balletic. It goes on for ages. Crockery is smashed, plants overturned, pictures pulled down from the wall and headbutted or drop-kicked out of their frames, wallpaper torn, chairs pulled apart, a plant-pot thrown through a window pane . . .

They continue until a banging on the door is heard. It might have been going on for some time.

Chris   If you don't open this door, I'm going to have to –

Miles   Shit, guys – the landlord.

Alistair   Leave him, door's safe. We'll let him in when we're –

The door flies open and **Chris** *is propelled into the room.*

For fuck's sake! Who did the barricade?

Chris *looks around.*

Chris   Oh my g –

Oh Jesus what have you –

What have you –

Toby *giggles, high-pitched.*

What the hell do you think you're playing at?

Alistair   Get him out, we're not finished.

Guy   You know what boys are like.

Chris *sees the smashed window.*

Chris   You've broken the –

Alistair   We said before we'd pay our way. You won't be out of pocket – show him the money.

Dimitri *comes towards* **Chris** *holding a wad of cash.*

Chris (*to* **Dimitri**, *pointing at* **Alistair**)   I want to talk to him.

Dimitri   OK, this is –

Chris   I don't want your money.

Dimitri   We made a deal.

Chris   I didn't make any deal.

Dimitri   Four hundred pounds? Earlier?

Alistair   Five hundred.

Dimitri   Sorry, five hundred. D'you remember?

Chris   That wasn't a deal.

Dimitri   I think there's a misunderstanding – we all saw you take the money,

Chris   Just for that one party.

James   Sorry, we thought you'd understood.

Alistair   For fuck's sake.

Chris   Don't start with me, my friend.

James   Look, here's what –

Chris (*to* **Alistair**)   You – What the hell d'you think gives you the right –

Alistair   You want to persist in being stupid?

Sit down.

Chris   I won't sit –

Alistair   Sit. Down.

Sit him down.

Harry *and* **Dimitri** *pick up a chair and lead* **Chris** *backwards to sit on it.*

George   Chaps. Let's all be – let's be gentlemen, shall we?

Chris   Gentlemen.

Alistair (*to* **Chris**)   Shut up and listen. This is what happens. You go back out there quietly and we do this and we pay you. We pay you a large amount of money – in cash – an amount of money that will well and truly cover the costs of your repairs, with something left over, most likely – which, by the way, is more than you'd ever get out of an insurance company. We pay you and we go away and everyone's happy.

Alright?

Chris   'Everyone's happy'? What you've done to my pub –

Alistair   Fuck's sake.

Alistair *takes the wad of cash from* **Dimitri**.

This. Is for you. OK? Whatever repairs you need, and plenty left over to take your daughter to Bicester Village, nice pair of shoes.

Chris   She doesn't want your money either.

Alistair *holds the cash close to* **Chris**'*s face. He looks at it.*

Alistair   Those are fifties, in case that helps the mental arithmetic you're doing right now.

Dimitri   We know how much it costs to do up a place like this, we've got experience.

Chris   People let you do this?

Alistair   If you're smart you'll take the treats and shut up.

Alistair *puts the wad of cash in* **Chris**'*s lap.* **Chris** *looks at it then brushes it off onto the floor.*

Chris   I don't want your money.

Alistair   Don't push me.

George   OK, guys, let's –

Chris   I don't want your money.

Alistair   Yes you do.

Chris *goes to stand up, but* **Alistair** *advances with menace, and he sits again.*

Yes you fucking do. It's the only reason we're still here, cause you know there's a fistful of notes coming at the end of the night.

Chris   Think you can buy your way out of anything, don't you? People like you think the world –

Alistair   Oh I know, you're torn up inside cause you think you don't like me. News for you, guv – you fucking love me, you'd like to *be* me but you can't quite admit it, can you? Chip on your shoulder much?

I mean what are you trying to do with this tawdry little cunt-shack? Private dining? What the fuck? Walking round like you own the place – but hang on, technically the *bank* owns the place, doesn't it? Have you paid off the loan for the conversion? No, thought not. (*re. the money*) This would do it, wouldn't it?

Now why don't you fuck off and let us finish the job?

Miles *and* **Ed** *have collected up the money from the floor, and put it back on* **Chris**'*s lap.*

Chris   Something happened to my daughter in here.

Alistair   Your daughter? What?

Chris   Very funny look on her face when she walked out of here a few minutes ago. Said you were playing silly buggers – some kind of kiss-chase thing, 'nothing to worry about, dad', but who's to say it wasn't more than that?

Cause if someone touched her inappropriately –

Harry   What are you alleging?

Chris   I'm saying maybe you assaulted my daughter.

Alistair   *Assaulted* her?

Chris   Ten of you in the room, innocent young girl?

Toby   No-one fucking assaulted your daughter.

Chris   I heard you, muttering obscenities earlier.

Toby   Me? What obscenities?

Chris   Something about 'pussy'.

Toby   Fuck's sake.

Chris   If any of you so much as tapped her on the shoulder –

Alistair   Mate, we wouldn't touch her with a bargepole.

Toby   Wouldn't fuck her with a bargepole.

Chris   You what?

Alistair   He said your daughter's a fucking slapper. I've got a room full of guys who saw her flashing herself about, total prick tease. You don't wear a black bra under a white shirt without meaning something.

Chris   You want a sexual assault conviction, the lot of you?

Dimitri   Sorry – *what*?

Chris   Follow you around your whole life, that will.

Toby   The fuck are you saying?

Chris   Cause that's not something you can pay your way out of.

Alistair *boils over, suddenly aims a swift uppercut at* **Chris***'s chin. It comes from somewhere deep and horrible.*

Chris *stands – it's unclear if he's trying to escape or fight back.* **Guy***,* **Harry** *and* **Miles** *all throw themselves at him, kicking and punching with fervour.*

Toby *lunges in, too.*

They stop when **Chris** *falls to the floor, unconscious.* **Toby**
*continues to kick him as the others stop, horrified, looking at what
they've done.*

George   Toby. Toby.

Toby *desists and takes a step back.*

The boys go quiet, looking at **Chris**. *Is he dead?*

Hugo   Fuck.

Guys?

Dimitri *goes towards* **Chris**'s *prone body.*

Guy   Is he OK?

James (*to* **Alistair**)   What the fuck are you doing?

Toby   Oops.

Alistair   He pushed me.

James   Is he breathing?

Dimitri   I don't know yet.

James   Jesus.

Ed *starts to cry.*

Dimitri   I don't know, does anyone know first aid?

Hugo   First aid? Need a fucking ambulance.

George   Find a pulse.

George *kneels down and listens next to* **Chris**'s *mouth.*

Ed   What have you done?

Toby   Shut up.

James   What if he dies?

Alistair   He's not going to –

James   He might. You beat the living shit out of him.

Alistair   He fucking pushed me.

Dimitri   OK, he's got a pulse.

Miles   Thank fuck.

Dimitri   Pretty faint, though.

Hugo *takes out his phone.*

Hugo   I'm going to call an ambulance.

Miles   Mate, please.

Toby   My dad is going to –

Alistair   Hugo, don't call a –

Miles *goes towards* **Hugo***, as if to snatch the phone, but* **Hugo** *steps back, holding up his hand.*

Hugo   Don't –

Alistair   Shit.

Hugo (*into phone*)   Ambulance, please.

Toby   Fucking hell.

Dimitri   Hang up hang up.

Hugo (*into phone*)   Yeah, the um, Bull's Head Inn, Kidsbury. Um, sort of a *disturbance*.

Ed   I want to go home.

Alistair   Man up, Eddie.

Hugo   Someone's unconscious –

Dimitri   Say he fell.

Hugo   Yeah, he – he fell –

How what? How did he fall?

Hugo *looks at* **Alistair**.

He got punched.

Guy   Fuck's sake, Tyrwhitt.

Hugo   No, it's um – fight's over.

Toby   Mate, seriously –

Hugo *looks at* **Chris**.

Hugo   I don't know, forties. I don't know him. He's the landlord. Yeah, he's unconscious now.

Dimitri   Give me the phone.

Hugo   OK. Yeah. Let me just –

Alistair   Give him the fucking –

Dimitri   Give me the phone.

Hugo   Fuck off! (*Into phone*.) No, not you.

Hugo *kneels down, checking if* **Chris** *is breathing*.

Yeah, he is. Yeah.

Yeah. Thank you.

(*To the others*.) On its way.

(*Into phone*.) Yeah, I'll stay on the line, OK.

Ed   Oh my god oh my god.

Dimitri *grabs* **Hugo***'s phone and hangs up*.

Hugo   She told me to –

Dimitri   Got to work out what we're going to say.

Alistair   Jesus, why the fuck did you have to –

Hugo   Ten of us in the room and none of us gets an ambulance, how does that look?

Dimitri   Should have talked about it first –

Hugo   And then maybe he dies while we're discussing –

Dimitri   They'll send the fucking police, mate – you told them there's been a fight.

Hugo   Fuck.

Alistair   Yeah, fuck. Yeah.

Ed   Shit, the police?

Dimitri   OK, let's just. We have to work out what we're going to say. Let's just think properly, OK?

Ed   Fuck fuck fuck.

Dimitri   Shut the door.

Guy.

Guy *goes and shuts the door.*

Put something there so –

Guy   Yeah.

Guy *wedges a chair under the door handle.*

Dimitri   OK. Now we think.

A long, painful pause. They really don't know what to do. The only sound, for quite a long time, is **Ed** *quietly sobbing.*

Anyone got a plan?

James   Toby – your dad's a lawyer, right?

Toby   No way. No fucking way.

Chris *emits a gurgling sound.*

Guy   OK, if he's making a noise he's OK, isn't he?

Miles   Let's just go.

Just walk out, they don't know who we are, we could climb out the window.

George   We can't just leave him.

Dimitri   They've got Hugo's number, mate.

Alistair   Brilliant.

Dimitri   Should have called from the fucking landline.

Miles   Shit.

Dimitri   If we'd fucking *talked* about it.

Harry *starts taking off his tailcoat.*

Harry   Take your tails off.

James   Why?

Harry   Cause if they know it's the club –

Ed *starts to take off his tails.*

Miles   I don't think they'll give a shit about what we're wearing.

Harry   If this becomes a thing, that's the club over, isn't it? If this is splashed all over every –

Alistair   We say nothing, OK. Absolutely nothing.

Guy   We stick together.

James   And all suffer the consequences?

Guy   We were all here, we're all, you know, involved.

Dimitri   I don't know how far saying nothing is going to get us – the evidence pretty much speaks for itself.

Alistair   Have you got a better idea?

Hugo   Self-defence. He came at us, fists all blazing, we were just defending ourselves.

Dimitri   Ten on one?

Hugo   We were drunk and scared.

Dimitri   Plausibility.

Harry   We stick together, get each others' backs.

Alistair   So we all say the same thing.

Hugo   We all go down together?

Ed   We'll get put in prison!

James   No, hang on. What about –

What about we give them someone? One person. Only one person goes down.

Dimitri   Yes – yes.

Alistair   What?

James   Best case scenario.

Alistair   What d'you mean?

Dimitri   I think the idea – is this right, Leighton? – is we all point the finger at one person, say it was them had the fight with the landlord.

Toby   What, how d'you mean?

James   Nine of us stay clean, only one of us goes down.

Dimitri   If it's a one-on-one fight, it doesn't have to be a gang thing.

Toby   What, who are we talking about?

George   What happened to looking out for each other? Isn't that what the club's for? You don't leave a man out in the field, it's not what we do.

James   We'll be able to help him, yeah? One man takes a hit for the team, the rest of us pay him back later, look after him, you know, proper brotherhood.

Toby   Who are we saying? Last in first out, or something?

Hugo   I think we should do it.

Alistair   Mate, think about it.

Hugo   Not really in the market for thinking right now.

Alistair   You want to get done for perjury?

Hugo   We won't get done for perjury.

Alistair   What, you're a lawyer now, are you?

Hugo   I'm a chap with holes in his pockets and no-one useful on speed dial is what I am. Look at me – I wouldn't last five minutes out there. I'm built for hiding in libraries. I belong at college. Not getting sent down for something I didn't fucking do.

The boys look around at each other.

Guy   So which, um, which one of us? To go down.

Hugo   I think it's pretty obvious, isn't it?

Toby   I didn't even throw the first –

Dimitri   Ryle. You want to volunteer?

Alistair   No. What?

Dimitri   Looks quite a lot like it's your fault, mate.

Hugo   You did punch him first.

Alistair   I wasn't the only person to punch him. And the rest of you wanted to, even if you didn't.

James   It was you got everyone wound up.

Alistair   What?

James   All that stuff he said. 'Fuck you, we're the Riot Club', all of that. 'Stop apologising'.

Alistair   I only said what every other fucker in here was thinking.

Ed   Incitement. It was incitement.

Alistair   Oh fuck off. What, you can't think for yourself?

James   I don't know how we got to a place where it's OK to do *that*.

Look, from a presidential perspective I think it should be you.

Alistair   You agreed – you all agreed.

James   I mean this is supposed to be a dinner, right? Not a rally.

Ed   Can I just say, I know I'm new here, but I think my brother would have told me if I was going to be expected to beat a man shitless.

Alistair   Fucking hell.

Dimitri   Is everyone on board?

George   I hate this.

Hugo   D'you get it, Tubes?

Toby   Yeah. Yeah.

Alistair   Fucking hell, Maitland – I went in to bat for you.

Dimitri   When they ask you, what you going to say?

Toby   Ryle did it.

Alistair   I defended you, for Christ's sa-

Dimitri   Anyone else?

Toby   Just Ryle.

Dimitri   Good man. Eddie, you're with us, yeah?

Ed   Yeah yeah.

Alistair (*to* **Toby**)   And you punched him too – fucking booted him in the –

Toby   Can't get a criminal record, mate.

James   Sticks to you for life.

Alistair   Lord Riot would be so proud.

Guy   Why can't someone sort this out?

Dimitri   They can't, mate. But we can. Yeah?

Alistair   Dimitri, you need to stop coercing people to – how fucking British d'you feel now, mate?

Hugo   Bellingfield?

Dimitri   Mate?

Guy   OK, yeah. OK.

(*To* **Alistair**.) Told my uncle there wouldn't even be trashing.

Alistair   Milo – you hit him as well, do the honourable thing.

Miles   I want to work in America. You can't do that with a record.

Alistair   That's it?

Miles   Jesus, I've only been in the club one night, I don't want to go down because of it.

Guy   I promise we'll look after you.

Alistair   Villiers – mate. Come on. You know this fucking stinks.

Dimitri   Ambulance on its way.

Harry   If I get sent down from college –

Alistair   *Mate?*

Harry   I'm sorry.

Alistair   Jesus fuck. You hit him too –

Harry   You're the only person who's going to say that, so –

Dimitri   George?

Alistair   If you say no, mate, they can't do it. They can't do it unless they've got everyone.

James   Balf, listen. We're going to be there for him, yeah? The rest of his life – next year, ten years' time, twenty. Any kind of shit hits the fan for him –

Dimitri   The rest of us swoop in and sort it out.

Alistair   Because back in the day we beat up a landlord and it made us brothers for life.

Hugo   We didn't beat up a landlord, Al. You did.

Dimitri   Man up and take it.

Alistair   We can think of something else, Balf.

Dimitri   We haven't got time.

George   They want to save you.

Alistair   They don't.

George   We're going to help him, right?

Hugo   Mate – of course.

George   Al, it's the club, isn't it?

Alistair   The fucking club! You know what this is? This is –

Brotherhood? Fuck off. You don't love each other, this isn't *love*, it's *fear*, you're pathetic, you're –

Proud of yourselves, are you?

Where's your *dignity*? Look at your faces. 'How do I weasel my way out of this?' Little boys in the playground. This is the best days of your life, is it? A bear pit, a dogfight dressed up as –

The door handle is rattled from the outside. **Alistair** *stops.*

Rachel   Dad? Dad, you in there?

The boys are still, listening. **Rachel** *starts to bang on the door.*

Have you got my dad in there?

If you don't let me in I'm calling the police.

Alistair *collects himself and opens the door.*

Rachel *comes in, sees* **Chris** *on the floor and goes to him.*

Alistair   I'll be having a smoke.

Alistair *goes out.*

An ambulance siren is heard approaching.

Blackout.

Scene Two

The gentlemen's club, as in act 1 scene 1. **Jeremy** *stands as*
Alistair *comes in.*

Jeremy   Alistair.

How d'you do.

Alistair   My lord.

Jeremy   Please! Jeremy. Title's no use when you're *modernising*.

Come – sit sit.

They sit down.

How's your father?

Alistair   Um. Alright, I think?

Jeremy   School together.

Alistair   Right.

Jeremy   Glad he's put all that FSA business behind him. Rotten
job, that.

Alistair   It was once the Independent got hold of it, yes. Ten
years ago now.

Jeremy   Little incident of yours won't drag it all up again, I hope.

Alistair   I don't know.

Jeremy   Your father worried about that?

Alistair   Among other things. Look, I've spent quite a lot of time
recently getting bollocked because of this – I've disgraced my
family, college, the university and now you're going to bollock me
on behalf of generations of ex Riot Club members, frankly I've
heard it all already so –

Jeremy   I haven't asked you here for a ticking off.

Alistair   You haven't?

Jeremy   Drink?

Alistair   Wouldn't say no.

Jeremy *pours two glasses of whisky.*

Jeremy   Water?

Alistair   Tiny slosh.

Jeremy   Ice?

Alistair   Never.

Jeremy   Good man. Cheers.

Alistair   Cheers.

Jeremy *drinks and sits back in his chair.*

Jeremy   Now, it's true of course we're not entirely happy about all of this – Bingham goes to the trouble of intervening, one had assumed his *guidance* would be listened to.

But the consequences for you clearly go further than a simple beasting, or whatever the weapon of choice is these days.

You're due back in court when?

Alistair   Next month.

Jeremy   The rotters turned you in.

Alistair   Yes. Looks like it, yeah.

Jeremy   You took one for the club.

Alistair   Sorry, did Guy ask you to see me?

Jeremy   Guy?

Alistair   Cause we're not allowed to talk to each other –

Jeremy   Afraid not, no. But then that would require a reserve of courage I'm afraid my godson simply doesn't have. Whimpered like a puppy when I saw him.

Alistair   He was quite sick in the night. I was in the cell next to him, I heard him crying.

Hats off, though, they all kept their stories straight right through till morning.

Jeremy   When they paid their little fines and fucked off.

Alistair   So if Guy didn't ask you – sorry, I'm really not sure why I'm here –

Jeremy   You're with Johnny Russell, right?

Alistair   Um. Yeah.

Jeremy   Gather he's looked after your family for some years.

Alistair   Since the FSA thing, yes. Dad trusts him.

Jeremy   He's a good lawyer. What's he advising, how to handle this?

Alistair   I don't think I should –

Jeremy   Oh now. Come on, what's the defence line?

Alistair   Russell thinks I should say I was bullied into it by the others. By the club.

That they scapegoated me. Which is pretty much the truth, so –

Jeremy   So you get off and the club goes down in flames, yes?

Alistair   Something like that.

Jeremy   Forgive me, would it not be better for all concerned if the club could be kept out of this?

Alistair   Better for the PM?

Jeremy   I'm not acting for the PM here.

Alistair   I don't see how the club could be kept out of it.

Jeremy   With the right lawyer, absolutely. Preserve your reputation *and* that of the club – see if we can't stop it getting to court entirely.

Alistair   A different lawyer?

Jeremy   I know a man – ex-member himself, as it happens. Very useful at sorting out club scrapes over the years.

Alistair   I think this is a bit more than a scrape.

Jeremy   You should have seen some of the others. Little incident from the 80s threatened to rear its head recently – something about a ball gag – our chap got it hushed up very effectively.

I'd like to bring him in on this. Obviously, I could talk to your father for you if it's awkward or –

I mean the important thing is making bloody sure that *you* come out clean.

Alistair   Keeping the club clean while we're at it?

Jeremy   As I say, he'll do both.

Alistair   No, then. Not interested.

Jeremy   I'm offering you –

Alistair   I don't give a shit about the reputation of the club – I'm not even *in* the club, why would I want to preserve it? Smash it – what's it good for?

Jeremy   You know, I suppose, that if you go that way we'll be obliged to come after you with all the might we can muster?

Paint you as an oddball, the delusional loner. People seem to understand that paradigm, don't they?

Alistair   You won't have to work very hard to make them dislike me.

Jeremy *sits back in his chair.*

Jeremy   Of course there's the other boys to think about.

Alistair   All got their own lawyers, they'll be fine.

Jeremy   They're all terrified, frantically trying to second guess what you're going to do.

It's a powerful position you're in. Imagine their relief if they didn't have to testify. Imagine the *gratitude*.

Alistair   I don't plan on seeing them again.

Jeremy   You might find that rather difficult – unless you're planning to leave the country, you might find your lives moving along rather proximate tracks.

Think about it – nine people pathetically grateful to you for the rest of your life.

Alistair   I'm sorry, I know what you're doing, trying to *manage* me. I don't need managing, I know what I think.

The club is fucking ridiculous. Rich little boys poncing around in tailcoats once a term? Just a bunker, isn't it? *Performing* something they haven't got the guts to be outside of the dinners. Like those fucking loons who dress up and do medieval battles. Reenactment.

Jeremy   Of course we know there's an element of silliness, letting off steam –

Alistair   Training up a generation for a life in hiding. So they can end up just like you – sneaking around, desperate not to get into the papers, denying the club ever happened. Pretending you're the same as everyone else – I'm sorry, I find it shameful.

Just going round in *disguise*.

Jeremy   Not disguise, no.

Alistair   What then?

Jeremy   I know how you feel, I've felt it myself. The first compromise you make winds you like a rugger ball in the stomach. Stays with you like school porridge. But the next time it hurts a little less, you learn to breathe into the pain and move along and each time it's easier.

Because by then you learn it's not simply disguise. It's *adaptation*.

Alistair   That's just a different word for –

Jeremy   No, it's not. It's survival. We adapt to *survive*.

It's what we've always done, it's what we'll continue to do.

You think the country's gone to the dogs and we're going with it, but you're wrong. You can't turn a ship around on a sixpence, you know? There's a longer game to be played.

My first club dinner they rolled me down a hill in a barrel full of prunes. Sick all over myself of course, laughable now, but the chap being rolled down the hill next to me, he pretty much runs the country now, and I'm not talking about the PM.

What I mean is, the dinners are just the beginning. The toasts, the scrunches, the high-jinks – a three-year initiation, if you like. Into something bigger, a group of people out in the world, making things happen.

You might have lost your place at college and at the dinner table, but you're still in the club. You can't afford not to be.

Jeremy *takes a business card out of his pocket and holds it out to* **Alistair**.

I'm not just offering you a better lawyer. I'm offering you a future. One pragmatist to another – it would be worth your while to take it.

Alistair *looks at the card.*

Alistair   I need to talk to my dad, to –

Jeremy   You're an adult now.

Alistair *takes the card.*

Good.

Alistair   Thank you.

Jeremy *pours another drink.*

Jeremy   You know you're not at all what I expected.

Rather thin on the ground, people like you.

Alistair   What, delusional loners?

Jeremy   Independent minds. Dangerous weapon you've got there.

Alistair   Can't turn it off.

Jeremy   Do you want to learn to use it to better effect?

Alistair   What d'you mean?

Jeremy   Well, why don't you come and spend some time at my office, see how we do things?

Alistair   I don't want anything handed to me on a plate just cause I –

Jeremy   I haven't offered you a constituency, Alistair.

Maybe you've got it in you to do something special one day. If that's the case, I'd rather you be doing it in my camp than in someone else's.

Jeremy's *phone buzzes in his pocket and he takes it out.*

My cue to go.

We'll talk again.

Alistair *puts his drink down.*

No no, please, don't get up. Stay and finish your drink, shame to waste it. Have a look around the building if you like. Not quite as fusty as it looks.

Jeremy *stands, goes to leave.*

Alistair   You loved it, didn't you?

Jeremy *is stopped in his tracks.*

Jeremy   What?

Alistair   You still love it, it's still in you. You say it's pathetic, just silly student japes. But you wouldn't have missed it for the world – the dinners, the toasting, the trashing. The Riot.

Jeremy *pauses, puts his hand on the back of his chair.*

Jeremy   Did you know the original spelling of Lord Riot's name, wasn't R-I-O-T, but R-*Y*-O-T? Two Ts, actually.

Alistair   No, I didn't.

Jeremy   Nothing to do with the idea of riotous behaviour originally. Don't know when the change happened, but there it is.

Thank god someone made the switch.

Jeremy *smiles at* **Alistair**.

Alistair   Could have just been a mistake.

Jeremy   People like us don't make mistakes, do we?

Jeremy *leaves.* **Alistair** *settles back into his chair and looks up at the portraits on the wall.*

Alistair *smiles.*

Blackout.

The End.

Notes

6   'Rugger' – Rugby.

8   'Day School' – Jeremy is asking because of the perceived superiority of independent boarding schools. At Eton and Harrow, pupils are resident; at independent day schools, pupils go home at the end of the day.

8   'Comprehensive' – a non-fee paying, non-academically selective school in the UK.

9   'Daily Mail' – a popular right-wing tabloid newspaper in the UK.

12   'Val d'Isere' – an expensive ski resort in the French Alps.

14   'Division Bell' – the signal for Members of Parliament to vote.

17   'dregsing' – A ritual punishment or ordeal, involving the 'offender' having to drink the dregs of other people's wine glasses, which have been adulterated with whatever disgusting substances as are available.

18   'Varsity' – the annual sports events between Oxford and Cambridge universities.

19   'The Fens' – a rural area near Cambridge in the East of England.

22   'the radius' – an apparent reference to the real-life ban of Oxford University dining clubs from organising events within a certain area of central Oxford.

23   'Magdalen Marys' – presumably a reference to Magdalen College (pronounced Maudlin), part of Oxford University.

25   'Harrow' – Harrow School, a fee-paying boarding school. A rival to Eton College.

31   'OUCA' – Oxford University Conservative Association. Linked to the UK Conservative party and formed in 1924, four previous prime ministers have been members in the past. It is pronounced 'owca', i.e as a single word

32   'Bristol' – Bristol University. Playing with the idea that Etonians are destined for Oxbridge.

34   'Kidsbury' – a fictional location but can be assumed to be on the outskirts of Oxford.

35   'The Great Escape' – a 1963 film which features Steve McQueen riding a motorbike.

35   'Port Meadow' – a popular green space for outdoor activities in Oxford.

38   'Cowes' – Cowes Regatta, a prestigious sailing event.

39   'Mahiki' – an upmarket night club in Mayfair, London.

42   'Alan Sugar' – British entrepreneur and host of the UK version of *The Apprentice*.

43   'economy went, well tits' – a reference to the 2008 global economic crisis.

47   'Sommelier' – a wine waiter.

54   'LMH' – Lady Margaret Hall, a college of Oxford University.

55   'Newky Brown' – Newcastle Brown Ale.

60   'Hugo, Guy and George' – Hugo has adapted a speech from Shakespeare's *Henry V*.

65   'For King and Country' – traditional battle cry of the English Army.

65   'Oh Captain, my captain' – reference to Walt Whitman's poem 'O Captain, My Captain'.

66   'Blackbird Leys' – Pronounced 'Lees' it is Oxford's largest council estate (public housing).

91   'William of Orange' – King William III (reign 1689-1702).

91   'National Trust' – British charity which focuses on heritage conservation.

93   'our lot are in power now' – a reference to the 2010 UK General Election.

94   'Goldman' – Goldman Sachs, a global investment banking company.

95   '95% mortgage' – reference to one of the causes of the 2008 global economic crash.

95   'New Labour' – reference to social economic policies introduced by UK Labour Party between 1997 and 2010, such as the minimum wage, New Deal and Welfare to Work.

96   'Bedfordshire' – a pun on the word 'bed'.

97   'sort it out' – reference to the 'Austerity' economic policies of the UK 2010 coalition government which involved cutting public spending.

99   'Wykehamists' – member or former member of the independent school, Winchester College.

101   'Athens burns' – reference to the Greek government debt crisis, a consequence of the 2008 global economic crisis.

104   'guillotined' – the execution of members of the French aristocracy during the French Revolution.

104   'last queen' – Queen Victoria (1837–1901).

105   'Why-aye' 'Howay the lads' – popular greetings in Newcastle, UK.

110   'sniffy' – line of cocaine.

117   'Bicester village' – Pronounced 'Bister' – a designer shopping centre on the outskirts of Oxford.

126   'Incitement' – in legal terms, the encouragement of another person to commit a crime.

128 'sent down' – expelled from university.
130 'FSA' – Financial Services Authority.
130 'Independent' – left-leaning, liberal newspaper in UK.
132 'PM' – Prime Minister.
136 'constituency' – the area for which a Member of Parliament serves.